Turkey

Berlitz Publishing Company, Inc.

Princeton   Mexico City   London   Eschborn   Singapore

Berlitz Trademark Reg. U.S. Patent Office and other countries
Marca Registrada

Text:	Stephen Brewer
Editor:	Media Content Marketing, Inc.
Photography:	Pete Bennett (except pages 49, 51, 57; Fred Mawer, Neil Wilson)
Cover Photo:	Pete Bennett
Layout:	Media Content Marketing, Inc.
Cartography:	Raffaele De Gennaro

Although the publisher tries to insure the accuracy of all the information in this book, changes are inevitable and errors may result. The publisher cannot be responsible for any resulting loss, inconvenience, or injury. If you find an error in this guide, please let the editors know by writing to Berlitz Publishing Company, 400 Alexander Park, Princeton, NJ 08540-6306.

ISBN 2-8315-7824-8

Printed in Italy
010/202 REV

CONTENTS

• A (☞) in the text denotes a highly recommended sight

Turkey

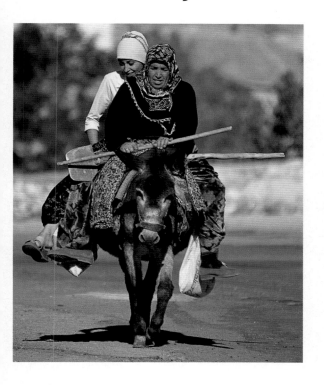

ON THE BEATEN PATH IN TURKEY

In Turkey, you are likely to be continually unsettled by the impression that something fascinating and mysterious is happening beyond every gate you pass or around the next bend in every road. Of course, given the very long and very rich history that has shaped this part of the world, one might say *has* happened. Rarely will you be misguided in this perception.

In İstanbul, climb the staircase outside the waterfront entrance to the Egyptian Bazaar and you will find yourself in Rüstem Paşa Cami, a small mosque. Often overlooked by visitors, it was designed by the great Ottoman architect Sinan and is awash in magnificent İznik tiles. At Termessos, on the Mediterranean Coast, scramble up a mountainside path, inconspicuous except for its steep pitch, and *Durun!* (that's Turkish for stop): Before you lies a vision-like theater perched spectacularly on the edge of a steep precipice. In Bursa, as in just about any Turkish town of any size, succumb to the urge to wander through the scent-filled lanes of the *bedestan* (covered market). You are in for something of a surprise, especially if you find yourself in this leafy, hillside city of mosques and tea gardens in July and September; at the center of the market is the Koza Han (cocoon hall), filled in those months with the fluffy commodities that will yield the city's famous silk.

Of the many such experiences that await you in Turkey, one more worth mentioning — and seeking out — is the pleasure of swimming from beaches at Patara, Olympos, Side, or Phaselis, raising your head from the warm Mediterranean waters, and looking back toward land to notice that the shore is littered with the remains of ancient, once-thriving cities: a ruined temple here, a granary there, a bath complex rising from the scrub. Then there's the somewhat unsettling sensation of looking over the side of a boat gliding over the waters of the Kekova Sound to see Roman mosaics and columns glistening beneath the waves.

You will drink very deeply from the well in Turkey, and to do so will require remarkably little effort on your part. The fact is, Turkey has accommodated the stampede of travelers — albeit, many of them donning armor and with conquest and plunder on their minds — for millennia. To experience the richness of this nation (a term that has applied to these former holdings of a succession of empire builders for well under a hundred years), you need only follow paths much beaten since ancient times.

Find yourself in İstanbul and you can't help but be overwhelmed by the ages-old spectacle of domes, minarets, street vendors, busy waterways, palaces, and all the other much-heralded notes of exoticism. For a particularly eye-filling dose of such a scene, take yourself to the middle of the Galata Bridge at sunset; you may also enjoy a similar view from the deck of a ferry on the Golden Horn or the Bosporus.

The drama of being in a fabled city that spans two continents and more than that many millennia, where

Women spin the wool that will be woven into exquisite carpets.

you can retreat from the crush of traffic to a harem garden cooled by a splashing fountain and where minarets are as much a part of the modern skyline as glass office towers, is one of the most profound experiences İstanbul offers its visitors. You're unlikely to soon tire of the spectacle of East meeting West that has been part of this city's appeal since its Byzantine heyday.

Prized Turkish carpets for sale in a Kalekory store.

Take time to wander along the busy streets of Taksim or Eminönü and simply observe. All the heady activity that swarms around you can, much too simply, be summed up as the phenomenon of modern Turkey. Growing recklessly, İstanbul now counts more than 12 million souls among its inhabitants, a number said to swell by as many as half a million a year as the unemployed from elsewhere in Turkey crowd into sparse and often makeshift housing. As the country turns increasingly to the West for economic growth, Turkey is also seeing a return to Islamic fundamentalism and traditional ways. What you will witness of these trends are sights and sounds of remarkable contrasts. The muezzin's call to prayer competes with honking horns and the crow of roosters; head scarves and veils are as commonplace as American and European fashions; the object of the ages-old ritual of bargaining is as likely to be a cell phone as it is a bag of saffron or a kilim (and sooner or later you will certainly find yourself on one side of the negotiating table).

From Turkey's largest city, you can follow ancient routes along the Aegean and Mediterranean coasts. The cities that proved so irresistible to conquerors like Alexander the Great still stand, a little the worse for wear but magnificent nonetheless. Legendary Troy, hilltop Assos, windswept Pergamum, marble-clad Ephesus—a traveler's itinerary along the Aegean coast takes in many of the great cities of the ancient world.

Just when you think you've exhausted all the ruins that could possibly lie scattered along any shoreline, round the bend at Bodrum (stopping perhaps to partake of the hedonistic pleasures of Turkey's most popular beach resort) and turn east. Another coastline, that of the Mediterranean, stretches before you; this one also cradles the remains of one ancient city after another, built by the Lycians and other long-gone civilizations: Kaunos, Xanthos, Myra, Aspendos. It's quite likely that you may have never heard of some of these ancient places or even of the people who settled them, a fact that makes their discovery all the more satisfying.

To help put things in perspective, stop in the thriving seaside city of Antalya and pay a visit to its museum, well-stocked with archaeological finds from local sites. A bit weary of these wonders of the ancient world? Relief is easy to come by. Antalya's old harbor is surrounded by cobblestone lanes lined with shops and cafés; the nearby beaches at İstuzu, Ölüdeniz, and Patara, all easily reached off the coast highway, stretch for miles; and the pleasant towns of Kalkan and Kaş provide the prospect of doing nothing more taxing than sipping a cool beverage on a wisteria-shaded terrace. Aside from the odd Lycian rock tomb or two, there's probably not a ruin anywhere in view.

When it comes time to turn your sights inland, what awaits you is Cappadocia. In this magical and mystical landscape, nature has conjured up whimsically conical mountains by way of countless volcanic eruptions. Over the years inhabitants have added an extra flourish by digging churches, monasteries, and entire cities out of the soft tufta, and this combined

The archway of Hadrian's temple is fronted by Corinthian columns—it dates back to the second century A.D.

effect of geology and human enterprise is nothing short of astonishing. Hike along a path that meanders through riverside copses, then climb a ladder into a simple, single-room church decorated with stunning eighth-century frescoes. This is one of those experiences any traveler wishes for and it qualifies as one more chapter in the annals of the mysterious discoveries that await you at so many places in Turkey. Another excursion takes you across the broad Anatolian plains to Konya, a former Selçuk stronghold that gave rise to the mystical order of the Mevlevi, the Sufi order we know as the Whirling Dervishes.

This, at least, is the itinerary we set out on the following pages. We leave many roads untraveled—the harsh landscapes of the far east; the Black Sea routes; and the streets of modern Ankara, the city that Atatürk made capital of the new Turkey when he became the first president of the Republic in 1923. We are confident that Turkey will indeed draw you back many times and that for now, İstanbul, the Aegean and Mediterranean coasts, and Cappadocia will fulfill the expectations of even the most ardent traveler.

A BRIEF HISTORY

At the city of Troy, a combination of myth and historical evidence suggest that more than 3,000 years ago the Greek soldier Odysseus rolled a large wooden horse through the heavily guarded gates and presented it as a gift to Paris, son of the king. The rest of the story, of course, is told in one of the great epics of Western literature, the *Iliad:* Soldiers crept out of the horse under cover of darkness, laid siege to the city, and freed Helen, Queen of the Spartans, whose face, it is said, launched a thousand ships. At Gallipoli, just a short distance north, in tragic circumstances that unfortunately are not laced with myth, more than 240,000 troops died during fierce fighting in the spring of 1915. At Pergamum and Ephesus, farther south along the Aegean coast, great libraries attracted the scholars of the ancient world. And at the city we now call İstanbul, at Konya and at Edirne, the Byzantines, the Selçuks, and the Ottomans established their respective empires, all meant to prosper for millennia (although none of which did).

With so many remarkable events of history rolling across its coasts, plains, and mountains, Turkey is rich in tales of intrigue, accomplishment, conquest, and glory, and the landscape is liberally littered with the remains of the places where these events transpired. For much of its long history Turkey has been at or near the center of the world.

A traveler, accordingly, can't help but feel blessed, and perhaps a bit humbled, to trod on turf that has nurtured both events of enormous magnitude and the countless unheralded, quotidian activities that account for the onward march of civilization. In Turkey you can climb the heights of the acropolis at Assos to catch a breeze and enjoy the view of the Aegean as Aristotle once did, or wander through the rooms of the Harem in Topkapı Palace and ponder the excesses of sultans. Beyond the many fabled ruins and great monuments are the vestiges of untold lives and unrecorded events: In Perge, you can walk along streets rutted with tracks left by cart drivers long vanished from the face of the earth and examine mosaics that adorn shops where merchants went about the not-so-extraordinary business of day-to-day commerce. In the once great cities of the long-vanished kingdom of Lycia along the Mediterranean Coast, such as Tlos and Xanthos, the ubiquitous rock tombs do not house the earthly remains of kings but of ordinary citizens whose deeds and misdeeds are for the most part lost to us forever.

Around 800 B.C., the Lycian culture began to flourish along the Mediterranean coast of Turkey.

Conquerors and the Conquered

The characters in the first chapter of this long and ongoing history include the Neolithic peoples who built settlements on the Anatolian plains some 9,000 years ago. By the second millennium B.C., the Hittites, who crossed the Caucausus and established a stronghold in Central Anatolia, were waging war against Egypt and Mesopotamia and the aforementioned city of Troy had already risen to prominence then fallen to the Greeks. Such seemingly unrelated events are among those that set the stage for the ongoing drama between conqueror and the conquered that has shaped so much of Turkish history.

Indeed, beginning in the eighth century B.C., wave after wave of invading armies and navies set their sites on inland plains and coasts alike. The Phrygians, under King Midas of the golden touch, flourished in inland Anatolia, and the Lydians, who invented coins and dice and were at one time ruled by the fabulously rich Croesus, settled in Sardis, near the Aegean Coast. Greek city states sprang up on the shores of the Aegean, and fell several times — first to the Persians who, in the sixth century B.C. under Cyrus II, expanded their empire into most of Asia Minor, and again in the fourth century B.C. to Alexander the Great. By the second century B.C., the Roman Empire had engulfed most of Asia Minor, and with the Romans came the

The whimsical landscapes of Cappadocia provided hidden refuges for early Christians.

relative calm and prosperity of the *pax romana*. In your wanderings up and down the Mediterranean and Aegean shores, you will come upon the baths, theaters, and monumental gates that suggest that, under Rome, attention shifted away from the field of battle to the enjoyment of leisure.

Early Christians to the Selçuks

Under the Romans, there was time to turn to spiritual pursuits, and Christianity began taking a tenuous hold across Turkey. St. Paul followed an itinerary that may well be the envy of a modern traveler, preaching at Alexandria Troas, Assos, Ephesus, Patara, Myra, and elsewhere in Asia Minor. St. John the Evangelist settled in Ephesus, allegedly in the

Land of faith: throughout its tumultuous history, Christianity and Islam have both flourished in Turkey.

company of the Blessed Virgin. Certainly some of the most drama-filled stories of the early Christians are those of Cappadocia, who found that the cave-riddled landscape was ideally suited to monasticism and to the construction of simple underground churches, of which more than 600 continue to impart a sense of spirituality.

By the end of the fourth century, Christianity was the official religion of a now-divided Roman Empire. The eastern

Historical Highlights

6500 B.C.	Neolithic peoples settle near Konya.
1250 B.C.	Fall of Troy.
1100 B.C.	First Greek settlers arrive on Aegean Coast.
800 B.C.	Phrygian, Lydian, and Lycian cultures begin to flourish.
660 B.C.	Byzantium, now İstanbul, founded by Greek colonists.
546 B.C.	Persians, under Cyrus the Great, invade.
334 B.C.	Alexander the Great conquers the Persians.
130 B.C.	Romans create province of Asia Minor.
20 B.C.–A.D. 180	*Pax Romana* brings prosperity.
A.D. 40	St. Paul begins preaching Christianity in Asia Minor.
325	Christian Council held at Nicaea (İznik).
330	Under Constantine, Byzantium, renamed Constantinople, becomes the capital of the eastern Roman Empire.
527–565	Emperor Justinian builds the Aya Sofya and other Byzantine monuments.
1071–1283	Selçuks establish an empire.
	Crusaders sack Constantinople.
1243	Genghis Khan lays waste to Selçuks.
1326	Osman lays foundation of Ottoman Empire in Bursa.
1453	Mehmet the Conqueror claims Constantinople for the Ottomans.
1520–1566	Süleyman the Magnificent leads Ottoman Empire to zenith of its power.
1571	In first major defeat, Ottoman navy is crushed at Battle of Lepanto.
1680–1775	Ottomans lose much of their European territory.
1826	Mahmut II slaughters the Janissaries, the Imperial Guard, who have become a serious threat to his throne.

1832	Greeks win independence from Ottomans.
1839–1876	Reforms sweep through Ottoman Empire.
1877	Young Turks help establish first Parliament, soon abolished.
1908	Constitution and Parliament restored.
1911–1913	Ottomans lose remaining European territories in Balkan Wars.
1914–1918	Turks fight in World War I as German allies.
1915	Turks repel Allies at Gallipoli, massacre Armenian civilians.
1920–1922	Greek army advances into Turkey and is repelled.
1923	Treaty of Lausanne establishes modern Turkey; Greece and Turkey exchange "minority" populations; Turkish Republic is established, with Atatürk as its president.
1925–1938	Atatürk carries out massive modernization programs.
1930	Constantinople officially renamed İstanbul.
1938	Atatürk dies. Turkey joins United Nations.
1950	Turkey becomes a multi-party democracy, though civil unrest and military coups persist into the 1980s.
1952	Turkey joins NATO.
1973	Bosporus Bridge links Europe and Asia.
1974	Turkey invades Northern Cyprus.
1980s	PKK launches guerilla warfare against Turkish government.
1997	Military forces pro-Islamic Welfare Party to step down, fearful of its fundamentalist leanings.
August and November 1999	Earthquakes kills thousands in northwest Turkey.
December 1999	Turkey becomes full candidate for EU membership.

The Library of Celsus in Ephesus was erected under the reign of the Roman Empire, in the second century A.D.

half was based in Byzantium, renamed Constantinople in honor of the emperor who ably ruled Asia Minor from the rapidly expanding capital. Affairs of the early Christian church took on great importance, prompting fractious debates over such matters as the divinity of Christ that were resolved at church councils in Nicaea, now known as İznik, and elsewhere. Byzantium flourished, especially under the emperor Justinian, who built the Aya Sofya and many of the other great monuments that grace the city today.

The riches and splendors of the Byzantine Empire proved to be irresistible to a new breed of invaders — Normans, Avars, Bulgars, and armies of crusaders were among those who moved across the frontiers with force, while the Venetians and Genoese made incursions into the state coffers with their trade along lucrative land and sea routes.

By the 11th century, the Selçuk Turks, warriors who traced their origins to the Asian steppes, were making inroads deep into the Byzantine Empire, bringing Islam with them. The 13th century saw the heyday of the Selçuks, who, administered by the Sultanate of Rum based in Konya, swallowed up the remnants of the Byzantine Empire. What remains of the *kervansarays* (inns), bridges, and roads they built across their holdings to accommodate increased trade along the Silk Route attest to the immense but short-lived power they enjoyed.

Enter the Ottomans

The greatest achievement of the Selçuks, as history would have it, was paving the way for one of the greatest empires the world would ever know, that of the Ottomans. From their early capitals in Bursa and in Edirne, the Ottomans slowly laid the foundations for the empire that would dominate Asia Minor and parts of Europe and Africa for much of the next six centuries. Over the next 200 years or so, the armies of one sultan after another planted the Ottoman standard on new territories. In 1453, Mehmet the Conqueror took Constantinople, renaming it İstanbul and converting the Aya Sofya to a mosque. By 1520, Selim I had brought Palestine, Egypt, and Syria under Ottoman control. From 1520 to 1566, the aptly named Süleyman the Magnificent had doubled the size of his empire, conquering widespread lands from northern Africa and Iraq to the Balkans and Hungary. Süleyman's achievements on the domestic front were equally impressive, and are most visible in the Süleymaniye Cami in İstanbul and the other mosques built by his architect, Sinan.

Decline and Fall

It is not possible to dwell on the Ottomans for too long without tipping the hat to the excesses that held sway at Tokapı Palace.

Indeed, Süleyman's offspring — at least those not disposed of by his ambitious wife, a former concubine named Roxelana — were rotten apples who fell very far from the tree. Selim II (known also as Selim the Sot), was a drunkard who drowned in his immense bath tub, but not before the Ottomans suffered their first significant naval defeat — and a massive one at that — losing 200 of their 245 ships at the Battle of Lepanto in 1571.

Little by little, under a succession of unenlightened and often debauched sultans, the Ottoman Empire began to crumble. By 1700 the Ottomans had lost most of their European holdings, and by the 19th century the empire was powerless to prevent Greece, Egypt, Lebanon, and other territories once in its firm grip from declaring independence. Despite some enlightened reforms instigated by Mahmut II and a burst of ostentatious palace building on the banks of the Bosporus, the last of the Ottoman sultans faced mounting challenges to their power; these included bankruptcy and growing opposition from within, most notably from a group of reformists who formed the Committee for Union and Progress (CUP), more popularly known as the Young Turks.

The empire, ironically geared at last to governmental and judiciary reform, lost more ground in the Balkan Wars of 1912–1913 and in the aftermath of World War I, in which Turkey sided with the Axis powers. Among the victims of the war, which saw the massive Allied defeat at Gallipoli in the spring of 1915, were some 1.5 million Armenians living in the Ottoman Empire. After the Armenians declared loyalty to Russia, men, women and children were rounded up and killed in a massive genocide.

Birth of a Nation

Turkey faced more turbulent years as the Allies moved in to parcel up what was left of the Ottoman Empire and more or less put Turkey under a state of occupation, called the Capitulations. Mustafa Kemal, a wildly popular Ottoman general and reformist, rallied nationalists to form an independence movement that drew up the so-called National Pact, establishing the borders of modern Turkey, and in April of 1920 held the first meeting of the Grand National Assembly. Despite the strength of the ground swell of support for the nationalists, the Allies continued with plans to partition Turkish territories; Greek armies, meanwhile, pushed eastward from the Aegean coast, finally meeting defeat at the hands of the Nationalists and forced to retreat to the sea at İzmir in the late summer of 1922.

In November the Grand National Assembly abolished the sultanate. On 24 July 1923, the Treaty of Lausanne was ratified, recognizing Turkish frontiers established by the Nationalists and calling for population exchanges under which, in

In Patara, a theater and other ruins scattered among sand dunes attest to a once-prosperous Mediterranean port.

**YURTTA BARIŞ
DÜNYADA BARIŞ**

K.ATATÜRK

1881-

reprisal for Greek aggressions, Greek Christians were exiled from Turkey to Greece and Turkish Muslims were sent from Greece to Turkey. Kemal, taking the name Atatürk (Father Turk), became president of the new Turkish Republic, and in short order ushered in changes that would undo centuries of tradition. Polygamy was abolished, alcohol legalized, education for women made mandatory, the fez and turban prohibited, dervish orders and other religious brotherhoods outlawed, the Muslim lunar calendar replaced with the Georgian calendar, and Arabic script replaced with Latin script for official communication.

In every Turkish town, monuments to Atatürk commemorate the great leader who introduced massive reforms in the early 20th century.

Into the Present

Turkey was suddenly in the 20th century, and in the maelstrom of world events. A pro-Western stance in the Cold War years brought membership in NATO in 1952. Turkey's invasion of Cyprus in 1974 resulted in economic sanctions and tensions that continue today. Membership in the European Union has been rejected twice and is still pending, though as of 1999 Turkey has been a candidate for full membership. On the domestic front,

Turkey has seen, on the one hand, the emergence of full-fledged multi-party democracy and, on the other, several military coups. While Turkey has made astonishing leaps into the here and now, especially in the past 20 years, industrialization and technological advances have been accompanied by such ills as rampant unemployment and runaway inflation. Even as the nation looks increasingly to the West for economic growth, the call from many segments of the population for a return to traditional Islamic values has become louder. The Kurdistan Workers Party (PKK) has gained the attention of the world press, declaring a guerilla war against the Turkish state and triggering military aggression in response.

If one single act can be said to galvanize attention on Turkey in recent years, it is the earthquakes in August and November of 1999 that claimed at least 20,000 lives. In its aftermath, support for the victims came from all political factions and from unlikely benefactors from abroad that included Greece, with whom Turkey uneasily shares a common border — proof that an act of nature can indeed be more forceful than the machinations of mere mortals.

The Süleманıye mosque in İstanbul is considered to be master architect Sınan's greatest achievement.

A Brief Who's Who in Turkish History

Croesus was the last of the Lydian kings, and at one time controlled the cities on the Aegean coast. He mistook the oracle who told him he would destroy a great empire if he attacked the Persians; he did attack, and he did destroy an empire, his own. Placed on a pyre in Sardis, he asked for divine intervention, and a downpour doused the flames.

Alexander the Great, endowed with strength, ambition, and luck, crossed the Dardanelles in 334 B.C., routed the Persians, and made his way down the Aegean and Mediterranean coasts, stopping at many of the now-ruined cities you are likely to visit.

Hadrian, Emperor of the Roman Empire from 117 to 138, made a state visit to the relative backwaters of Asia Minor — an event that is notable mostly because you will find monumental arches built to honor the occasion in Antalya and elsewhere.

Osman captured Bursa in 1326, laying the foundation of the empire that would take his name — Osmanli, or Ottoman.

Süleyman the Magnificent lived up to his name, managing during his long sultanate (1520–1566) to double the size of the Ottoman Empire, prove himself a just administrator, and with the help of his architect Sinan, build some of the empire's greatest monuments, including the Süleymaniye mosque complex in İstanbul and the Selimiye Cami in Edirne. Unfortunately, he wasn't as wise in his choice of a favorite wife, Roxelana, an ambitious former concubine who convinced the sultan to murder his son Mustafa; her own son Beyazit; and Ibrahim Pasa, his son-in-law, grand vizier (prime minister) and closest advisor — all in the interest of promoting the succession of her sodden, half-witted first born, Selim.

Atatürk, Turkey's favorite son, was born Mustafa Kemal into a lower middle class family in 1881. Even before he became President of the Republica and earned his new name, which means "Father Turk," he had repelled the Allied attack at Gallipoli and led the revolutionary movement that overthrew the Ottoman sultanate. He was just as effective in a peaceable role, introducing massive reforms that included suffrage and education for women. He died of cirrhosis in 1938, amid the gilded Ottoman extravagances of Dolmabahce Palace.

WHERE TO GO

Mosques, minarets, bazaars stacked high with spices, ancient ruins washed by turquoise waters, churches aglow with frescoes — the mere mention of Turkey launches a seemingly endless stream of exotic images, all of which tend to be accurate. Nowhere does the vast richness of this nation that straddles Europe and Asia come to light more vividly than it does in İstanbul, the mesmerizing city that plants itself solidly on both continents.

We begin our travels here, with the knowledge that this city only whets the appetite to see more. So, from İstanbul and its environs we proceed along the history-etched Aegean and Mediterranean coasts, then move inland to the magical landscape of Cappadocia.

İSTANBUL

The name, from the Greek *eis tin polin,* or "to the city," says much about the enduring allure and vast importance of İstanbul. There were many centuries when anyone, anywhere in the world, would refer to "the city" and be understood to mean this fascinating metropolis that has, throughout the ages, been known as Byzantium, the New Rome (when it became the seat of the Eastern Roman Empire in A.D. 330), and, well into the 20th century when President Atatürk introduced sweeping reforms to bring Turkey into the modern age, as Constantinople. The city witnessed the passing of Greeks, Persians, and early Romans, flowered in the sixth century under the Emperor Justinian, who built the Aya Sofia, the church/mosque that crowns the city to this day, and rose from ruin and neglect in the 16th century, when the Ottoman Sultan Mehmet II set about building mosques, monuments, and a magnificent royal enclave, the Topkapı Palace.

All this historical intrigue may seem a bit daunting, and the city's stunning setting on the hilly terrain of two continents, bisected with boat-choked waterways, is almost guaranteed to disorient the newcomer. Monuments, scents, and the omnipresence of the exotic are so overpowering in İstanbul that even the most earnest traveler will often be tempted to abandon the tight timetable and decided itinerary. İstanbul is a city to savor at leisure, whether by pausing to catch another glimpse of the minaret-pierced skyline or by sitting down with a carpet dealer for your umpteenth glass of apple tea. Begin in Old Stambul, where a staggering wealth of sights are within easy reach of one another, then venture across the Golden Horn on the Galata Bridge into modern Beyoğlu and the other sections of this city that sprawls, picturesquely, along both sides of the Bosporus.

Old Stambul

Here, in the old town, you can view countless artifacts in some of the city's finest museums, step into some of the world's most hallowed religious structures, wander through room after room of the Topkapı palace, view ancient ruins, barter at İstanbul's acclaimed bazaars, dine at the bottom of a Roman cistern, and perhaps sleep in a finely restored Ottoman house. You can do all this quite comfortably, because Old Stambul is relatively small and easy to navigate on foot.

☛ Aya Sofya

Above Old Stambul — and more precisely, above the historic neighborhood at its heart, **Sultanahmet** — rises Aya Sofya, or Church of the Holy Wisdom. From the time of its completion under the Emperor Justinian in 537, Aya Sofya was the largest and most important church in the Christian world. This magnificent structure quickly assumed similar stature in the Islamic world, when the Ottoman sultans appropriated it

The elaborate Blue Mosque was built to overshadow the grandeur of Aya Sofya, but doesn't.

as a mosque 900 years later, adding the four minarets. Today, Aya Sofya serves as neither church nor mosque, because Atatürk converted the structure to a museum in 1936.

Contributing in no small part to the overpowering presence of Aya Sofya is its dome, which was not eclipsed in size until Saint Peter's rose in Rome 1,000 years later. In designing the dome, Byzantine architects accomplished the impossible — the massive structure seems to float over the interior of the church, an illusion created by using hollow bricks made of lightweight, porous clay.

Once inside this massive building, you are less likely to be overwhelmed by its size than by its intimacy, due in part to the warm hues of the stone, and by the luster of its **mosaics,** many commissioned by the Emperor Justinian to ensure that his church would be the most splendid in Christendom. In the 16th century, Süleyman the Magnificent followed Islamic law forbidding representation of man or animal and ordered the mosaics to be covered. Fortunately, workers did so with plaster that inadvertently provided a protective coating.

Ongoing restorations continue to reveal the sheer splendor of these works, many in gold, portraying saints and angels; two of the most important show the Madonna and Child, and Christ flanked by the Virgin Mary and John the Baptist. For a look at more secular images, walk to the far end of the south gallery, where the 11th century Empress Zoë improvised a convenient way to portray a secession of husbands — when one would pass on, she would simply have the image of his face replaced with that of his successor. On view for the ages is Constantine, who outlived his wife. The most popular corner of Aya Sofya is that, in the north aisle, housing the so-called Weeping Column; according to legend, the moisture that gathers on its brass- and marble-clad surface will cure any number of ailments.

The Blue Mosque and Surroundings

The presence of a building as perfect as Aya Sofya presented a challenge to 16th

Ever upward point the minarets of the Blue Mosque as seen from the Hippodrome.

century Sultan Ahmet I, who commissioned a mosque within its shadow to rival it. You can be the judge of whether he succeeded, but whatever you decide, you are likely to be mesmerized by the Sultan Ahmet Cami, better known as the **Blue Mosque.** As you enter from Sultanahmet Square, pass through the main gate and forecourt, and step through the side doors (only the faithful can walk through the massive main portal), you will find yourself standing beneath a canopy of airy domes and six minarets. The space is bathed in the light of 260 stained-glass windows and aglow with 20,000 blue İznik tiles (so-called for the ceramics-manufacturing city just south of İstanbul; see page 55).

Several buildings surrounding the mosque once housed shops, alms houses, and other establishments oriented toward servicing the faithful. One of them is now the **Mozaik Müzesi** (Mosaic Museum), which shelters a magnificent stretch of mosaics that once paved the pathway leading to a long-ruined Byzantine Imperial palace. Not uncovered until the mid-20th century, the mosaics are in splendid condition and colorfully depict flora, fauna, scenes from mythology and, with some degree of pomp, the occasional emperor or two. Another amazing collection is housed in the nearby **Hünkar Kasrı** (Carpet and Kilim Museums). Should you be inspired to possess such a carpet for yourself (and you probably won't be leaving Turkey without at least one tucked under your arm), you may want to step into one of the several shops in the covered arcade near the entrance to the Mosaic Museum.

Just opposite the Blue Mosque is the **Hippodrome,** site of the 100,000-seat stadium that for much of İstanbul's history hosted chariot races, circuses, and other entertainments; mass assemblies; and an occasional spurt of public violence. It was here, in 1826, that Sultan Mahmut II oversaw the slaughter of the Janissaries, his dangerously powerful and disloyal royal guard. Though the actual structure has not fared as well as Rome's Coliseum, many of its monuments continue to grace a large greensward at the center of what was once the chariot track. These include the Serpentine Column, pirated from the Temple of Apollo at Delphi, and an obelisk that the Byzantine emperor Theodosius appropriated on his conquest of Egypt. No longer here are four bronze horses that the Crusaders, returning from the Holy Land, pillaged and took to Venice, where they are now part of the treasury of San Marco.

Under the Byzantine and Ottoman empires, the Aya Sofya and the Blue Mosque were surrounded by the sumptuous palaces of the powerful elite. You can step into one of them, the **Ibrahim Paşa Sarayı** (Ibrahim Paşa Palace), on the western edge of the Hippodrome. This 16th-century stone mansion and the furniture, carpets, and other holdings of the Turk Ve Islam Eserlei Müzesi (Turkish and Islamic Arts Museum) that fill its rooms, provide a satisfying look at Ottoman lifestyles. You'll also learn a bit about the ill-fated tenant for whom the palace is named, a one-time confidant of Süleyman the Magnificent who fell out of favor and was strangled.

> A sign you'll see outside mosques: *Lutfen ayakkabilarinizi cikartiniz* (Please take off your shoes).

The Archaeological Museum and Topkapı Palace are nearby, and you can reach them by walking back across Sultanahmet Square. You'll want to pause to take a good look at the massive bulk of Aya Sofya as you pass, and you may also want to step into the **Yerebatan Saray Sarnici,** one of the many cisterns the Byzantines built, often expanding earlier Roman constructions, to ensure that the city would be supplied with fresh water during sieges. Colored lights and piped-in music lend a somewhat ersatz air to this vast underground space, but the columns and elaborate arches reflected in the rippling waters produce an eerily fascinating atmosphere nonetheless.

You may be overwhelmed by the many layers of history you encounter in İstanbul, and the Arkeoloji Müzesi (Archaeological Museum) will help you put things in perspective. An exhibit on İstanbul history nicely explains the city's Greek, Roman, Byzantine, and Ottoman past, and gathered here are the best examples of statuary and other artifacts from Troy, Ephesus, Aphrodisias, and the many other important archaeological sites throughout Turkey. This complex also includes the **Eski Şark Eserleri Müzesi** (Museum of the Ancient Orient), which houses, in rather unremarkable displays, some astonishing artifacts, including clay tablets inscribed with the law code of Hammurabi. The nearby **Cinili Kosku** (Tiled Pavilion) was built in 1472 as an Imperial residence and was fittingly covered in colorful tiles. Only portions of them remain, and a large collection of İznik tiles, similar to those used in the Blue Mosque, are on display inside.

Topkapı Palace

The name **Topkapı Palace** (Topkapı Sarayı) suggests wealth, pleasure, and intrigue, all of which this enormous residence and administrative center of the sultans has sheltered over the years. The alluring maze of ornate, jewel-filled state rooms, fountain-cooled gardens, and the famous harem, set on a lovely hilltop overlooking the confluence of the Sea of Marmara and the Bosporus, is a pleasure to explore.

The various palace pavilions and living quarters are clustered around four courtyards. You'll cross the first one, the **Court of the Janissaries,** to reach the ticket office. This large open space was the precinct of an elite corps of guards serving the sultan. They were Christian by birth, recruited as young boys from the Balkans, and trained to be soldiers. Janissaries, however, were far more than a professional army — well-educated in Islam and civic affairs, they filled some of the highest posts in the palace, ensuring that the sultan was surrounded by loyal retainers. The Ottoman mint (now a civic museum) is in this courtyard, as is the humble but ancient Aya Irini Kilisesi (Church of Saint Irene), now a concert hall.

After you pass Bab-ı-Selam (Gate of Salvation), you'll find yourself in the Second Court. The palace kitchens line one side. Aside from two rooms that have been reconstructed to give some idea of the atmosphere that prevailed when a staff of hundreds prepared meals for the palace's 4,000 residents, the various sculleries and oven rooms now display porcelain and glassware. You'll notice a disproportionately large collection of Chinese celadon dinnerware, a court favorite because it allegedly turned color upon contact with poisoned food.

The **Divan-ı-Humayum** (Imperial Council Chamber) is also known as *kubbealti* (literally, beneath the cupola), because it is topped with a distinctive cupola-like tower. In this hall the Grand Vizier met with the Council of State, more familiarly called the "divan" because members reclined on the couches that line the walls. These

Rulers watched the goings-on of the **kubbealti** *through this screen, known as the "Eye of the Sultan."*

proceedings were sometimes observed by the Sultan from behind a screen known as the "Eye of the Sultan." The many-domed **Inner Treasury,** one of several halls housing the most valuable of the famed Topkapı treasures, displays an extensive collection of arms and armor.

The **harem** is an intriguing warren of apartments and courtyards, incorporating about 400 rooms in all (of which you can visit about 40 on mandatory guided tours, some-times given in English). Life here was neither licentious nor, for most of the inhabitants, particularly enjoyable; however, true to the meaning of the word harem, or forbidden, what transpired here was shrouded in mystery, and residents of the complex had little or no contact with the outside world. Aside from the Sultan's mother (the Valide Sultan) and his official wives, who lived in luxury, the harem also housed, in conditions akin to slavery, hordes of eunuchs, concubines, and ladies in waiting.

The İftariye (Golden Cage) was actually a prison. In it lived brothers and other close male relatives of the sultan who might be in line for the throne. Confined here, they could cause little trouble and, limited as their lives were in this pleasure dome, they were likely to have little access to treasonous plots. The practice was an improvement upon the widespread fratricide in which sultans once engaged to ensure their place on the throne.

Much of the harem, especially the apartments occupied by the Valide Sultan and sultan himself, are appropriately and sumptuously domed and tiled. The most extravagant room in the harem, though, is the Hunkar Sofrasi (Imperial Hall), where the sultan entertained his preferred visitors.

While the harem was where intimacies of day-to-day life at the Ottoman court transpired, the Third Court was the Sultan's official domain. Here, beyond the Bab-ı-saadet

(Gate of Felicity), he received state visitors in the ornate kiosk known as the **Arz-Odasi** (Audience Chamber) — he would converse with them only through the Grand Vizier, as a Sultan would not deign to speak directly to anyone but a highest ranking member of his court. The Third Court also houses the **Treasury,** where you can view the palace's lustrous collection of eight-pound emeralds, the 84-carat "Spoonmaker" diamond (so-called because a peasant allegedly traded the gem for three spoons), and room after room of other jewels and jewel-encrusted swords and garments.

The **Fourth Court** is the most pleasant and relaxed precinct of the palace, laced as it is with gardens, summer houses and pools. The Sünnet Odasi here is a richly tiled pavilion in which young princes were circumcised. Two unusually elaborate kiosks to which Sultans would retreat to catch a breeze and look out over the city are also in this court: the Rivan Köskü and the more ornate Bagdat Köskü. You may want to linger in the Fourth Court for awhile, and you can do so either on one of the terraces overlooking the city and waterways below or in the pleasant restaurant.

The Bazaars to Süleymaniye Cami

Topkapı Place sits high above the workaday quarter of Eminönü. This waterside neighborhood bustles with crowds coming and going from the Bosporus ferries, the Sirkeci train station and the Galata Bridge. The **Egyptian Bazaar** (Mısır Çarşisi), also called the Spice Market, is just a few steps from the ferry docks. Stacked high with bags of spices, nuts, and dried fruits, this market opened for business in the 17th century to generate revenue for the Yemi Cami (the New Mosque) next door. The small **Rüstem Paşa Cami** (Rüstem Paşa Mosque), up a flight of steps in front of the waterside entrance to the bazaar, is more impressive, and in fact may well be the most beautiful mosque in İstanbul. The façade and interior are covered entirely in İznik tiles that are arrayed in a distinctive circular pattern.

The Grand Bazaar

The Egyptian Bazaar is only a fraction of the size of the **Grand Bazaar** (Kapalı Çarşi), where 4,000 shops selling all manner of merchandise, from mops to mint-condition antiques, line a covered warren of 65 streets. The streets between the two covered markets are clogged with vendors' stalls, handcarts transporting sacks of spices, and all manner of exotic hubbub.

Two recent fires, one in 1954 and another in 1974, have come close to destroying the bazaar, but restorations have retained the tiles, ironwork, and other elements of the original Ottoman style, including its 18 distinctive fountains. The

All kinds of Turkish treats are available in rich abundance at the Grand Bazaar in İstanbul.

A tea vendor outside of the Grand Bazaar wears traditional dress and carries his livelihood on his back.

bazaar is, by all rights, the world's first shopping center and grew from a small warehouse built under Mehmet the Conqueror in the mid-15th century to incorporate a neighborhood devoted to commerce, supplied by Turkey's position on the so-called silk routes between Europe and Asia. Merchants decided to connect their establishments with arcades, and eventually the huge complex was gated.

It's likely that you will lose your bearings in the maze of little lanes, so be prepared to wander randomly, and you'll probably also fall under the spell of this exotic marketplace and emerge with a purchase or two. Some particularly interesting precincts are the old bazaar, at the center of the complex, where dealers specialize in antiques and fine jewelry, and the Old Book Bazaar, which is outside the main market and just to the west.

Beyazit and Süleymaniye Cami

The busy square known as Beyazit is just to the west of the main entrance to the bazaar. On the south side of the square are the gates to what is now **İstanbul University,** occupying somewhat formal and austere buildings that face a mall planted with plane trees. At one time the buildings housed the Ottoman war ministry. The site has a long history — the forum of the Byzantine emperor Theodosus, built in A.D. 393, stood here, as did a wooden palace built and occupied by Mehemet the Conqueror before he moved his court to Topkapı Palace. Mehemet then used the palace as a sort of retirement home for elderly ladies of his harem.

The most ambitious of the Ottoman builders, the sultan Süleyman the Magnificent, is best remembered in İstanbul for his eponymous mosque, **Süleymaniye Cami,** just north of the university. The mosque is the largest in İstanbul and is one of the city's favorite and, given its prominent location on a hill overlooking the Golden Horn, is one of the most visible landmarks. Considered to be the highest achievement of Sinan, Süleyman's master designer, Süleymaniye Cami is austerely beautiful, with a vast dome supported by four columns and elegant proportions that lend a spiritual air to the space. Süleyman and Sinan are both buried on the grounds.

West to the Walls

The streets immediately to the west of Süleymaniye Cami lie in the shadow of the **Aqueduct of Valens,** begun in the fourth century as part of the extensive system of reservoirs, cisterns, and waterways that ensured that the city would be supplied with water during times of siege. A little farther west is yet another vestige of the city's early history, the enclave of Fatih. This term means "the Conqueror," and the Fatih monument commemorates the conquest of İstanbul by Mehemet the Conqueror in 1453. He is buried next to the **Fatih Cami** (Fatih mosque), the first to rise above Ottoman İstanbul. The original structure and its attendant schools and almshouses were leveled in a 1776 earthquake, and while the mosque that stands in its place has never been completed

The Ottoman leader Süleyman the Magnificent is entombed at his eponymous mosque.

(the interior is largely undecorated), it serves quite efficiently as the center of a large and devout religious community.

Eyüp Sultan Cami and Environs

One of the most hallowed sights in İstanbul is often overlooked by the city's non-Muslim visitors. **Eyüp Sultan Cami,** in fact, is the holiest site in Turkey, and among Muslim pilgrimage sites, only Mecca, Medina, and Jerusalem are more visited. This mosque complex on the western end of the Golden Horn (and easily reached on one of the Golden Horn ferries that leave from the Eminönü side of the Galata Bridge) entombs Eyüp Ensari, the standard bearer of the Prophet Muhammad who was killed carrying the Islamic banner during the seventh-century Arab siege of Constantinople.

The tomb was already a revered monument when Mehemet the Conqueror built a mosque to commemorate Eyüp in the

15th century. Rebuilt in 1800 after an earthquake, the mosque and tile-covered tomb are reached by a series of peaceful, shaded courtyards. So important is this relatively modest mosque to the Islamic faithful that for centuries Ottoman princes came here to assume the role of Sultan. In keeping with these noble associations, the tombs of many Ottoman notables surround the complex.

Another remarkable structure at this end of the Golden Horn is Stefi **Stefan Bulgar Kilesi** (Church of Saint Stefan of the Bulgars). The presence in İstanbul of this non-Greek orthodox church, once the center of a thriving Bulgarian community, is notable in itself, but Saint Stefan is also one of the most unusual structures in a city with no shortage of remarkable architecture. The interior and exterior are constructed entirely of cast iron, and the church was actually built in Vienna in 1870 and shipped in pieces to İstanbul on more than 100 barges.

> **The crows of roosters aren't the only sounds to pierce the dawn in Turkey. You'll also hear the *ezan*, the Muslim call to prayer.**

Nearby, and directly west, are two remarkable remnants of Byzantine İstanbul. The city's western boundaries are entirely walled in, from the Golden Horn to the Sea of Marmara, with the fortifications that Theodosius II started in 413. When the walls were destroyed by an earthquake in 447, a work force of more than 65,000 civilians, much of the able population of the city, rebuilt them in just two months, barely completing the job before the legions of Attila the Hun reached the city and were successfully repelled.

The former church of the Holy Savior, now known as the **Kariye Müzesi,** is practically within site of the walls. The magnificent fresco cycles here are considered to be the finest extant examples of Byzantine art and present a highly emotional and detailed account of the life of Christ.

New İstanbul

Across the Golden Horn from Old Stambul is the "new" section of the city, often referred to as Beyoğlu, which is actually the name of one of several neighborhoods that climb the hill from the shores of the Golden Horn and the Bosporus. There were settlements here long before Christ, and this part of İstanbul is new only in the sense that in the 19th century many Europeans and Western-oriented Turks chose to settle on this side of the water rather than in the starchy confines of Sultanahmet. Many of the buildings, especially those in the fashionable district of Pera, are of European rather than Ottoman design, and a good number of shops, cafés, and other establishments cater to Western tastes. It's only fitting that the relatively few modern high rises in İstanbul are clustered around Taksim, the commercial center of the new city.

The best way to approach the new town is by foot, crossing the Golden Horn on the **Galata Bridge.** Pause midway across to take in the view. Behind you, Topkapı Palace is perched on its promontory to your left, the domes and minarets of Aya Sofya and the Blue Mosque fill the horizon directly in front of you, and the massive dome on Süleymaniye Cami is to your right. The buildings of the new town climb the hillside ahead of you, with the golden roof of the cylindrical 14th-century Galata Tower rising above them.

Karaköy

At the foot of the bridge you can board an underground train for the short trip to Tünel Square and from there continue to Taksim. Although this railway is quite historic — it was built by the French in 1835 to provide European residents with an easy way to commute to and from their waterfront offices and hillside residences — you should forego the ride and set off on a walk that is bound to provide you with a rewarding glimpse at little snatches of Turkish life. Karaköy, as this waterfront district is known, was the province of European traders during the Byzantine and Ottoman empires. It is still a seaport, with shipping offices, chandlers, and docks that serve Bosporus ferries and ocean-going vessels.

Just inland from the bridge you will cross Voyvoda Caddesi, named for the 15th century prince (voyvoda) of Transylvania who is more familiarly known as Count Dracula. There is no apparent connection between the street's namesake, a fierce enemy of the Ottoman regime whose severed head was brought to the city from Romania and put on public

The 14th-century Galata Tower rises above the so-called "new city" and the shores of the Golden Horn.

display, and its 19th century prominence as the banking center of the empire.

Galata Tower to Pera

A few blocks up Yüksek Kaldırım Caddesi is **Galata Kulesi** (Galata Tower), part of a 14th-century fortifications network built by the Genoese, one of the many powers who have trammeled the shores of the Golden Horn. In the shadow of the tower are several synagogues, some established more than 500 years ago by refugees from the Spanish Inquisition. In 1986, Arab gunmen burst into one of them, Neve Shalom, and opened fire, killing 22 members of the congregation.

Galipdede Cadessi continues up the hillside through an intriguing neighborhood of narrow alleyways and stepped streets. A few steps up the street you'll come to **Divan Edebiyatı Müzesi** (Museum of Divan Literature), a former monastery of the sect known in the West as Whirling Dervishes and now a museum of calligraphy and Dervish memorabilia. The distinctive whirling dance, which is said to induce a trance-like spiritual state, is performed the last Sunday of every month at three in the afternoon.

Tünel Meydani (Tünel Square) is just north of the museum. This pleasant plaza, surrounded by shops and cafés, is the northern terminus of the underground railway from Karaköy. It is also the southern end of the tram line that runs up and down **Istiklai Caddesi** (Independence Street) between Tünel and Taksim squares, but you'll want to travel this main street of the new town on foot.

Until the early days of the last century, Independence Street was known as the Grand Rue de Pera, and in its smart shops and cafés European residents of the surrounding **Pera** neighborhood could outfit themselves in Parisian finery, enjoy French pastries, and comport themselves as they would at home. Many of the mansions and palaces that line the street once housed the embassies of long-since abolished empires whose representatives in İstanbul doggedly engaged in diplomatic struggles with the last of the Ottoman sultans. Now that the capital is in Ankara, many of the former embassies house foreign consulates, and the flags of many different nations flutter over Independence Street. These imitation palazzi and chateaux are Western in style, no doubt reflecting the determination of their colonial-minded inhabitants to stake a claim for a world far removed from the mosques, marketplaces, and other exoticism that surrounded them. Rising above this architectural hodgepodge and adding to the neighborhood's general sense of geographic displacement are the steeples and crosses of Anglican, Dutch Reform, and other churches.

Another European stronghold in İstanbul is the **Pera Palace.** Built in the 1890s to billet passengers traveling between Paris and Constantinople on the Orient Express, over the years this Belle Epoque hotel has compiled a guest roster that includes Mata Hari, numerous royals and statesmen, and Agatha Christie. The latter wrote *Murder on the Orient Express* here, and her room and the one once occupied by Atatürk have been cordoned off for public viewing. A ride in the birdcage elevator and a sip of tea in the Edwardian salon are experiences unique to İstanbul.

To Taksim

About halfway up Independence Street, a more Turkish atmosphere asserts itself on the alleys and arcades that branch off **Galatasaray Meydanı** (Galatasaray Square). The square itself is one more bulkhead of European İstanbul, named as it is for the looming edifice that dominates it, a former lycée where Ottoman children were schooled in French and in Western manners. In the **Çiçek Pasajı** (Flower Market), just off the square, floral displays are tended by an equally colorful corps of loquacious vendors. There are those who will tell you that this market is not what it once was — that is, before 1978, when the glass dome and other parts of the structure came crashing down, necessitating a thorough renovation. The adjoining **Balık Pazarı** (Fish Market) shows no such signs of modern incursions, and its famous fishmongers, standing behind their voluminous displays of the daily catch and engaging in the age-old art of cajoling customers, are no small part of the market's appeal.

The main function of **Taksim Meydanı** (Taksim Square), at the northern end of Independence Street, appears to be accommodating a constant flow of traffic that streams around its few notable landmarks. The Atatürk Kültür Merkezi (Atatürk Cultural Center), the city's main concert hall, is here, as is the Cumhuriyet Aniti (Republic Monument), erected during the 1920s celebratory fervor surrounding Atatürk's establishment of a Turkish democracy. Surrounding the vast square are the unofficial, and somewhat dispiriting, landmarks of modern İstanbul — a cluster of banal office towers and Western-style hotels.

> Never photograph anyone without first asking his or her permission.

Beşiktaş

Eventually, the royal inhabitants of Topkapı Palace followed the wave of Westernization and moved across the river as well, building palaces here on the banks of the European shore. Despite the lavishness of these last residences of the sultans, the mirrored and gilded interiors reflect not prosperity but the fading days of the Ottoman Empire.

Dolmabahçe Palace

Sultan Abdül Mecit commissioned **Dolmabahçe Sarayı** (Dolmabahçe Palace) on a spot along the Bosporus that in the 17th century had been filled in and planted with imperial gardens (Dolmabahçe means "filled-in garden"). The sultan intended the move to be a sign that he was willing to unwrap the Ottoman Empire from the mysteries shrouding

A ferry ride along the Bosporus is an enjoyable way to view the extravagant Dolmabahçe Palace.

Topkapı Palace and would spare no expense in bringing his rule up to date.

Dolmabahçe, however, proved to be a white elephant from the day the dissolute and soon bankrupt sultan moved his court here in 1854. Gilded in silver and clad tastelessly and excessively in marble, the palace is an ornate extravaganza that would long outlast the crumbling empire it was meant to reinforce. Ironically, the democratic-minded Atatürk lived here in the last days of his presidency. He died in one of the palace's simple rooms in 1938, on the morning of 10 November at 9:05am, a time you will probably note because the palace clocks have been stopped to mark the exact hour.

Çirağan Palace and Yıldız Park

Abdül Mecit's brother, Abdül Aziz, had far fewer funds to draw upon when in 1863 he built his own showcase just up the river, the smaller and relatively modest **Çirağan Sarayı** (Çirağan Palace). The palace is now part of a luxury hotel set in extensive riverside gardens. Just across the river and practically within sight of Çirağan, Abdül Aziz also built a smaller (a mere 30 rooms), but no less ostentatious palace, **Beylerbey Sarayı.** He also lavished attention on a royal garden that is now **Yıldız Park,** a leafy hillside refuge just above Çirağan where his harem was allowed to roam the paths and enjoy the kiosks and pleasure pavilions in relative freedom.

In the 1880s the park became less secluded when Sultan Abdül Hamit II commissioned the 62-room **Yıldız Şale** (Yıldız Chalet) to accommodate visiting foreign dignitaries. The sultan eventually established himself here as well, and among the memorabilia you will see on a tour of the small palace are some of the furnishings he made and the tools he used to craft them. Another collection in the park is that of the **Askeri Müzesi** (Military Museum), concentrating on more than 600 years of Ottoman campaigns and defenses. Among the most colorful displays are the many *sayebanalari,* the elaborately woven tents that sheltered sultans and other royalty on the battlefield; they appeared at victorious battles that ranged across the eastern Mediterranean into Asia Minor and Africa. Among the armor and weaponry is an extraordinary curiosity, what is alleged to be fragments of the chain that the last of the Byzantine armies stretched across the Golden Horn in a vain attempt to thwart an Ottoman sea attack during the Battle of Constantinople in 1453.

> **Looking for a cheap ride? Find the nearest dolmuş stop. These shared taxis run between fixed points in larger towns and cities.**

Along the river between Dolmabahçe and Çirağan palaces is one more show of Ottoman military might, the **Deniz Müzesi** (Maritime Museum). Dry-docked here is an

extraordinary fleet that includes imperial caiques and Ottoman war galleys, and other memorabilia ranges from can-
nons to mementos from Atatürk's yacht.

Along the Bosporus

The Bosporus cuts a broad swath through İstanbul, and love of
this storied river runs deep in the heart of every resident of the
city. Providing a direct artery between the Black Sea and the
Sea of Marmara, the Bosporus has been a vitally important
shipping lane since antiquity. Dividing European İstanbul
from Asian İstanbul, the river is also one of the city's major
thoroughfares, crisscrossed by millions of ferry-borne com-
muters every day. The Bosporus is so much a part of İstanbul's
long history that it is rich in
the city's earliest mythologi-
cal associations. Jason and
Ulysses allegedly sailed its
course, and the river takes its
name from Bous (cow) and
Poros (crossing place), a ref-

> The most common way to
> travel long-distance in
> Turkey is by bus; a driver's
> assistant will dispense cool
> drinks and moistened tissues
> during the trip, and will
> make frequent rest stops.

erence to an incident in Greek legend in which Zeus turns his
lover, Io, into a cow and his wife, Hera, spitefully conjures up
a gadfly to sting the beast and force her into the stream. Aside
from its legendary and historical importance, the river is also
lovely, and a boat trip upstream from the Eminönü docks provides rewarding views of waterside mosques and fortresses,
colorful villages, and the distinctive wooden villas known as
yalis, all backed by forested hills.

Once a quaint fishing village, **Ortaköy** is today an enclave
of brightly painted wooden houses and the favorite retreat of
well-dressed urbanites who partake of the almost carnival-
like atmosphere on summer evenings and gather in sidewalk
cafés. A far less secular sight is elegant Ortaköy Cami, these

Bazaars, Mosques, Museums, Other Sights

Arkeoloji Müzesi: Tuesday–Sunday, 9:30am–4:30pm; $3.

Askeri Müzesi: Wednesday–Sunday, 9am–5pm; $2.

Aya Sofya: Tuesday–Sunday, 9:30am–4:30pm; $5.

Blue Mosque: Daily, 9am–5pm (limited entry at prayer times); Free.

Deniz Müzesi: Wednesday–Sunday, 9am–5:30pm; $1.

Divan Edebiyati Müzesi: Tuesday–Sunday, 9:30am–4:30pm; $2.

Dolmabahçe Sarayı: Daily except Tuesday and Thursday, 9am–4pm; $5.50 or $10, depending on length of guided tour.

Egyptian Bazaar: Monday–Saturday, 8am–7pm.

Eyüp Cami: Daily (limited entry at prayer times); Free.

Fatih Cami: Tuesday–Sunday, 9am–5:30pm (limited entry at prayer times); Free.

Galata Kulesi: Daily, 9am–8pm; $1.

Grand Bazaar: Daily, 8:30am–7pm.

Hünkar Kasrı: Daily, 8:30am–3:30pm; $1.50.

Ibrahim Paşa Sarayı: Tuesday–Sunday, 9am–5pm; $3.

Kariye Müzesi: Thursday–Tuesday, 9:30am–4pm; $2.

Mozaik Müzesi: Wednesday–Monday, 9am–4pm; $1.50.

Rüstem Paşa Cami: Daily, 9am–5:30pm (limited entry at prayer times); Free.

Sadberk Hanim Müzesi: Thursday–Tuesday, 10am–6pm; $2.

Stefi Stefan Bulgar Kilesi: Daily; Free.

Topkapı Sarayı: Wednesday–Monday, 9:30am–4:30pm; $4 admission; harem tour, $2.

Yerebatan Sarnici: Daily, 9am–4:30pm; $3.

Yıldız Sale: Wednesday–Sunday, 9am–4pm; $1.

days overshadowed by the Bosporus Bridge. **Arnavutköy,** a former Greek settlement, is just upriver. This is a far quieter town, and its atmospheric waterfront is lined with beautifully preserved wooden houses.

Neighboring **Bebek** is one of the city's wealthiest enclaves, but Bosporus University and an attendant intellectual community lend the town a Bohemian air. The most impressive of many lavish waterside villas here is the Art Nouveau-style **Hıdıv Sarayı** (Khedive's Palace). The town's famous landmark is the far more imposing fortress of **Rumeli Hisari,** massive fortifications assembled by Mehemet the Conqueror in 1453 as he made his way down the Bosporus in his successful campaign to take Constantinople. Across the river, and completing the pair of sentinels overlooking this narrow stretch of water, rises another early Ottoman castle, **Anadolu Hisarı.** The next two villages, **Emirgan** on the European side and **Kanlıca** on the Asian side, also mirror each other from their opposite river banks. Each is famous for its local specialty — Emirgan for tulips, which bloom in a hillside park, and Kanlica for yogurt, served in several waterfront cafés.

One of İstanbul's finest art collections lies at the end of a river cruise, that of the **Sadberk Hanım Müzesi,** in Büyükdere. Turkish carpets, tiles, archaeological artifacts, and other pieces amassed by one of Turkey's wealthiest businessmen, the late Vehbi Koç, fill the rooms of two waterfront houses.

AROUND İSTANBUL

Within easy reach of İstanbul are peaceful islands, historic cities and even thermal spas. Some are places to relax, others to dig deeper into the past; all afford a rewarding glimpse into Turkish life.

The Princes Islands

Wealthy Turks build their holiday homes on the lovely Princes Islands.

As consuming as İstanbul is, even a visitor is likely to feel the urge to escape to a quieter retreat. The Princes Islands, only 20 km (12 miles) offshore in the Sea of Marmara, have been providing a place of escape for centuries, though some notable residents — political dissidents and an exiled Leon Trotsky among them — have not sought their restful beaches and forests by choice. Since the mid-19th century, the nine small islands have lured well-to-do city dwellers, and today, even a steady influx of summertime visitors who sail over from the Bostancı or Kabataş docks for a few hours don't distract from the islands' rugged beauty and considerable charm. Most refreshingly, the islands have been spared both modern development and motorized traffic; visitors explore them on foot and bicycle or in horse-drawn carriages.

Büyükada is the largest and most visited of the islands, and its devotees have built many wooden mansions surrounded by lush gardens. Trotsky lived in one, on Çankaya Cadessi in the main town. The island's most notable structure, topping one of its two hills, is the monastery of Saint George, which dates from Byzantine times and once served a community of Greeks who

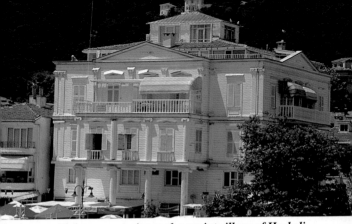

Make an excursion to the quaint village of Heybeli, in the Princes Islands.

sought refuge on the island. Its three chapels and alleged healing fountain are still of great importance to Orthodox Christians who make pilgrimages here, especially at Greek Easter.

Heybeli, the other large island of the group, is less developed and more rugged, and its wooden houses are a little more modest than those of Büyükada. The island's main attraction is also Greek Orthodox, the School of Theology, though its famous collection of Byzantine manuscripts is not open to the general public. A monastery on the island, that of Panaghia, is largely in ruin. Of greatest interest to most visitors are the island's lovely, untrammeled beaches.

Edirne

A road has led from İstanbul to Edirne since Roman times, and in its paving stones, bridges, and roadside stops the Via

Egnatia still occasionally bears traces of the Imperial legions, Byzantines, Ottomans, and conquering forces who have traveled its length. Edirne, 235 km (146 miles) northwest of İstanbul on the E80 toll road, lies near the modern Greek border at the heart of the ancient, war-prone region of Thrace. Despite these ancient roots, the city owes most of its outstanding monuments, especially its remarkable mosque, to the Ottomans.

The city, then known as Hadrianopolis after the emperor who made the outpost the capital of Roman Thrace, was the Ottoman capital beginning in 1361, and it was from here that Mehemet the Conqueror staged his conquest of Constantinople. Long after Edirne lost its luster as capital, sultans continued to retreat here to hunt and relax in royal splendor.

The **Selimiye Cami** dominates the city, as well it should. This beautiful mosque, begun in 1569, is the largest and finest in

Turkey, and in building it the great Ottoman architect Sinan set out to surpass Aya Sofia in majesty. By all appearances he succeeded. The dome, supported on eight columns set unobtrusively into the walls, creates a stunning celestial effect and, more than 45 m (150 ft) in diameter and almost 30 m (100 ft) high, is indeed larger than that of Aya Sofia, if only by a hair.

At 71 m (223 ft), Selimiye Cami's minarets are the highest outside Mecca.

Inside, exquisite tile work, 999 windows, and lacey stone-work imbue the massive space with light and serenity. Outside, four airy minarets surround the dome, levitating the entire structure heavenward. The mosque's collection of calligraphy, as well as ceramics and furnishings from throughout Thrace, are on display in the adjoining **Türk-Islâm Eserleri Müzesi** (Museum of Turkish and Islamic Art). You will also see many displays devoted to the more earth-bound art of yagli gures (oiled wrestling), a very popular pastime in Edirne. In fact, a statue of two practitioners of this centuries old art — which earned its prominence in local lore when 40 springs allegedly erupted on the spot where two of Süleyman's soldiers expired when wrestling in an encampment outside of town — presides over Hürriyet Meydanı, Edirne's main square.

The aptly named **Eski Cami** (Old Mosque) predates its more impressive neighbor by almost two centuries and, though its beauty derives from the simplicity of the square plan, its walls are covered in elaborate calligraphy. Eski Cami is at the center of the old city, and is therefore surrounded by the evocative evidence of Edirne's importance as a trading center on the Ottoman silk routes: the domed, 16th-century *bedestan* (market), the larger and recently renovated **Ali Paşa Bazaar,** and the **Rüstempaşa Kervansaray,** which continues to house travelers as it has for more than four centuries. The most impressive of the scanty remnants of the Roman city, **Kule Kapısı** (Tower Gate) looms near the entrance to the bazaar. A third historic mosque in Edirne, **Üç Serefeli Cami** (Mosque of the Three Galleries), is just north of the markets and is named for the balconies circling its graceful minarets.

One more burst of Ottoman monument building, the **Beyazit Külliyesi** (Beyazit Complex) is just north of the city, on an island in the willow-lined river Tunca and reached via the gracefully arched and two-tier **Beyazit Bridge.** From

The Turkish bath is an important local custom — and one that visitors are welcome to share.

midstream the 15th-century complex, the largest of many such charitable institutions built throughout the Ottoman empire, is especially remarkable, as hospitals, schools, storehouses, and the mosque are clustered beneath a sea of domes. The most evocative of the buildings here may well be the *timarhane,* or madhouse, quite enlightened for its time, in which peaceful gardens and splashing fountains were intended to soothe the inmates.

Termal

For millennia, the weary have soaked their tired bones in baths fed by hot springs that gush from beneath this pleasant village, some 185 km (112 miles) south of İstanbul, and most easily reached by ferry from İstanbul to Yalova, which is 12 km (7½ miles) east. Aside from some pleasant gardens

and the quaint cottage to which Atatürk used to retreat, the
only attractions in Termal are its public bathing establishments; while the Sultan and Valide Baths provide an ornate
ambience, the Kurşunlu affords its patrons the opportunities
to soak in outdoor pools then, wrapped in towels during the
cooler months, sun themselves on a large terrace.

İznik

It takes a little imagination to evoke the days when this lakeside farming center, 60 km (37 miles) south of Yalova, was
an important and famous place. In A.D. 375, what was then a
Roman outpost known as Nicaea hosted a council of the
early Christian church that proclaimed the Nicaean Creed,
establishing the doctrine that Christ is not inferior to God the
Father. In 787, the town hosted another council to pronounce
the doctrine of Iconoclasm, holding that icons were not to be
banned but were to be worshipped not for themselves but for
the holy figures they represented.

The short-lived Nicaean empire ruled a good part of the
Mediterranean world from here in the 13th century, and the
city, renamed İznik, achieved notice two centuries later
when its craftsmen, many imported from Persia, began shipping their famous tiles throughout the Ottoman Empire.
Unfortunately, the famous tiles are not much in evidence in
İznik. A few originals are on display in the **İznik Müzesi**
(İznik Museum), alongside ancient coins, jewelry, and some
remarkably well-preserved Roman tombs. The surroundings
are quite fascinating, as the museum occupies a former
imaret (hostel) built in 1388 to feed and shelter the poor.

The **Yeşil Cami** (Green Mosque) is across the street, and
its elegantly proportioned, one-room plan dates from the
same period as the imaret and is typical of the Selçuk style;
the green tiles that cover the minaret are not the originals

of İznik manufacture, which were replaced long ago. An even more evocative structure is the church of **Sancta Sophia** (Holy Wisdom). Though quite decrepit, this quaint structure is still endowed with its original fifth-century floor and wall mosaics. Scant Roman remains provide even earlier traces of the city's history: **Lefke Kapısı** (Lefke Gate) was built in A.D. 120 to celebrate a visit by the Emperor Hadrian, but rubble and a few entry arches are all that is left of the Roman theater.

Bursa

To see some of Turkey's finest examples of İznik tiles, you need only travel about 80 km (49 miles) south to Bursa. This busy, garden-laced city, famous for silk production and for its mosques and tombs, climbs the slopes of Mount Uludağ.

Yeşil

This hillside neighborhood, just above the city center, is named for its two famous monuments. The **Yeşil Cami** (Green Mosque) is considered to be one of the great Ottoman masterpieces, and no small part of its beauty derives from the blue and green tiles that adorn most of the interior spaces. Especially beautiful tiles decorate the sultan's loge, just above the foyer, and white marble etched with feathery designs covers the elegant entranceway.

The nearby **Yeşil Türbe** (Green Mausoleum) houses the grandiose sarcophagus of Sultan Mehmet I Celebi and members of what appears to have been his very large family. The exterior is covered in blue, not green, tiles of not particularly impressive quality; they are 19th-century replacements, installed after extensive earthquake damage. The interior, however, is awash in a sea of brilliant green, imbuing this final resting place with an air of serenity. The adjoining

Yeşil Bursa (Green Bursa) and Uludağ mountain, from the park of the city's Hisar, or fortress.

Bursa Etnoğrafya Müzesi (Bursa Ethnographic Museum) also displays exquisite tiles, along with its collection of Ottoman weaponry and household objects.

The presence of so many monumental Ottoman works in Bursa is a reflection of the city's role in the nascent Ottoman Empire. In the 14th century, Osman Gazi, the leader of a nomadic tribe, laid siege to Bursa, though it wasn't until the reign of his son, Orhan, that the city fell. Orhan proclaimed himself sultan, and the unified empire that began to flourish under his capable stewardship became known as Ottoman, from Osmali, the people led by Osman. The tombs of Osman and Orhan are near the walls of the ancient citadel that fell into Orhan's hands. To celebrate his victory, Orhan built **Orhan Gazi Cami,** the first city's Ottoman mosque that still graces the old center.

Other Mosques

Among the city's other mosques are two that seem to belong to the realm of the dead. **Emir Sultan Cami,** just east of Yeşil Cami, rises from the midst of graveyards popular with the devout, and Sultan Murat II Cami, in the medieval Muradiye district, is surrounded by the tombs of **Sultan Murat II** and members of the royal family, few of whom died peacefully in their beds; many were the victims of fratricide, murdered to keep them from interfering with a smooth succession. The 17th-century **Osmalı Evi** (Ottoman House) across the street is a museum that provides a look at how the well-to-do embraced the here-and-now.

Bursa's largest mosque, **Ulu Cami,** is enmeshed in legend — its 20 domes are allegedly a compromise that Sultan Beyazit struck when he couldn't fulfill his vow to build 20 mosques if he was victorious in battle. The fountain beneath the center dome is yet another compromise, made necessary when a 14th-century homeowner refused to sell her property to make room for the mosque. The presence of the fountain precludes any possibility of praying on land not donated willingly.

The Old Center

The mosque is at the edge of Bursa's old commercial district, where the 14th-century *bedestan* (covered market) winds through a confusing warren of little streets and cabinet makers, ironmongers, and goldsmiths ply their ages-old trades. At the center of the marketplace is the Koza Hanı (Silk Cocoon Hall), occupied by silk merchants who ply the trade that has fueled the city's economy for 600 years. In late June and July, silk breeders fill the hall with the feathery white commodities they sell in the cocoon auction.

Bursa's other great annual event is a November festival cele-brating Karagöz, the shadow-puppet theater that originated here in the 14th century. Local lore has it that Karagöz, a stone mason, and Hacivat, his foreman, broke the tedium of their labors on Orhan Gazi Cami by entertaining their coworkers with humorous, often ribald skits. The pair became such a popu-lar distraction that Sultan Orhan had them beheaded. Regretting his harsh cruelty and missing the pranksters, the sultan arranged to have them immortalized as shadow puppets — Karagöz as a black-eyed, turbaned knave and Hacivat as his hapless cohort.

THE AEGEAN COAST

The Aegean coast of Turkey has been a cultural crossroads for more than three thousand years. Greeks migrated here in the first millennium B.C. and laid the foundations for its mar-velous cities. In succeeding centuries, the Persians rolled in from the east; Alexander the Great's army marched down from the west; the Romans added the area to their vast empire; Arabs attacked from the south; the crusaders estab-lished military outposts; the great Ottoman empire took root; and climactic World War I battles were waged. Today, it is the geographic border of Turkey's uneasy alliance with the West. Turkey's Aegean Coast thus offers the traveler an unparal-leled picture of the past, in a setting of lovely beaches and towns, imposing ruins, and moving battlefield sites that com-bine into an experience that is hard to match anywhere else.

Çanakkale

Çanakkale is situated at the mouth of the Dardenelles, the narrow strait separating Europe from Asia. Known in the Classical Age as the Hellespont, these dangerously surging waters have proved irresistible to romantic swimmers — in ancient times, Leander swam them by night to visit his lover,

Hero, and the English poet Lord Byron repeated the feat in 1810. They have also proved strategically irresistible to centuries of armies — the Persian Xerxes crossed them via a bridge of boats in 480 B.C., on his unsuccessful campaign to conquer Greece, and Alexander crossed them going the other way 150 years later, on his (successful) march into Asia. In World War I, one of the bloodiest campaigns of this bloodiest of wars was waged just across the straits at Gallipoli.

Today, the town is a fairly utilitarian agricultural center. Its Army and Navy Museum, set in a 15th-century fort about a mile from the town center, holds a comprehensive display of ancient and modern weaponry, and provides a fine view of the Dardanelles and the Aegean Sea.

Gallipoli

Çanakkale is also a convenient departure point for a visit to the **World War I battlefields** of Gallipoli. Here, in the spring of 1915, Allied forces launched a massive campaign against Turkish troops to gain control of the straits and, ultimately, İstanbul. In the months of fighting that followed more than 160,000 Allied troops and 80,000 Turkish troops were killed. By Christmas, the Allied troops had retreated in defeat.

Tours to Gallipoli leave from Çanakkale; you can also take the car ferry and explore the region on your own. Carefully tended cemeteries and other monuments to the dead mark the former battlefields on the peninsula. An information center at **Kabatepe** is just to the south of the main sites, and this is a good starting point for a contemplative walk through this singularly peaceful and sad area.

Troy

The road to Troy, Route E87, runs 32 km (20 miles) south from Çanakkale, and the ruins of this legendary city lie just to the west, near the sea. Where some ancient sites amaze with their splendor or astonish with their grandeur, the remains of Troy are a far more modest affair: Parts of the massive East Wall and gate still stand, a paved chariot ramp leading into the city is intact, and trenches and foundations mark the streets and houses of the ancient town. To stand on the ramparts of this rocky outcrop and look over the Troad plain to the sea, where the thousand ships of King Agamemnon laid siege to Troy, is to experience a moment out of the literature that has shaped the West.

The Iliad

Homer's story, told in *The Iliad,* is familiar: Paris, son of King Priam of Troy, abducted Helen, wife of Menelaus of Sparta, and took her back to Troy where she was received as his wife. Menelaus immediately enlisted the aid of his brother, the great King Agamemnon, and together they amassed an army to get

The small port is but half of the Aegean city of Behramkale — the ancient city of Assos crowns its hill.

Helen back. For ten years, the Greeks, including Achilles, Hector, and Odysseus, tried to conquer the city. Finally, Odysseus hatched a scheme — the Greeks would present the Trojans with a gift of a great wooden horse and pretend to retreat. But the horse was hollow and filled with Greek soldiers; that night, as the Trojans celebrated their victory, the soldiers crept out and opened the gates to the invading Greek army.

So the story goes. It was long believed to be myth, but in the 19th century a German businessman named Heinrich Schliemann began excavations at the site and uncovered nine layers of remains of a prosperous city that had stood on the site for at least 4,000 years, including evidence that a battle took place at about the time of *The Iliad.*

The artifacts and jewelry that Schliemann found are long gone, first spirited away to a museum in Berlin by Schliemann himself, then stolen by invading forces after World War II. The cache is now in Russia; other objects recovered later are in İstanbul and Ankara. You'll need a guide or a good archaeological guidebook (available in the shop at the entrance), to make sense of the ruins, but it's well worth the effort and will provide an excuse to read one of Western literature's great epics.

Alexandria Troas

This formerly splendid city, 32 km (20 miles) south of Troy on Route E87, is the Ozymandis of the Aegean Coast: founded in the third century B.C. by one of Alexander's generals, it once encompassed a thousand acres, controlled much of the traffic between the Aegean and the Dardanelles, served as capital during the rule of the Romans, and was famous for its temple and baths. What remains today is a field, flowery in the spring, of crumbling walls and shards of pottery, with a fine view of the sea and the island of **Bozcaada.**

Behramkale

Called **Assos** in ancient times (and sometimes today), this is a divided city: Half of its inhabitants live around the imposing ruins, set on a hill, and the other half live in the small port below. It thus encompasses the two chief characteristics of Turkey's Aegean Coast — remains of the past and lovely harbors and coves.

Assos, 50 km (30 miles) south of Alexandria Troas, may have been a Hittite settlement in the 13th century B.C., but its true rise began in the eighth century when settlers from the Greek island of **Lesbos** took root here. They constructed a terraced city, much of which remains, set on an impregnable site above Aegean shipping routes. In the fourth century B.C., Hermias, a former student at Plato's Academy in Athens, rose to power and instituted a regime based on the Platonic notion of the philosopher-king. He began a school of philosophy, attracting no less than Aristotle, who eventually married the niece of Hermias. After his execution by the Persians, the city passed from one ruling power to the next; the medieval Ottomans did considerable damage when they dismantled the ancient town for building stone.

The view from the top of the ancient **acropolis** is wonderful — down the coast, and over the Aegean to the Greek Island of Lesbos. The sixth-century B.C. **Temple of Athena** still stands, at least partially; an American archaeological team is currently restoring the original Doric columns. Around it is a collection of ruins, what remain of the ancient agora, gymnasium, and theater — all essential components of a classical city. The necropolis is well preserved, strewn with pieces of the limestone sarcophagi for which ancient Assos was famous, and about 3 km (2 miles) of the old city walls are intact. A curiously modern note is struck by the 14th century **Murad Hüdavendigar Cami,** a simply proportioned mosque.

The harbor lies at the bottom of a steep road. It is a compact collection of restaurants and hotels; since the Greeks are encamped only 8 km (5 miles) away, at Lesbos, it also has its own border police.

Ayvalık

Follow the coast road around the Gulf of Edremit to the charming city of Ayvalık, 131 km (81 miles) south of Assos. Founded by Ottoman Greeks in the 16th century, it was a prosperous and ethnically Greek city through the succeeding centuries, but it was left all but empty after its inhabitants were ejected from Turkey in 1923, after the Greek-Turkish war. It's since been resettled, but it still feels Greek: The houses are square stone structures (as opposed to the tall, narrow houses more typical of Turkish architecture), and the mosques are mostly former Greek Orthodox churches.

The picturesque city of Ayvalık — still an important fishing port — retains the feel of its 19th-century heyday.

The heart of Ayvalık still looks like a 19th-century city: Its narrow, winding streets, overhung with balconies and lined with lovely carved wooden doorways, form a maze through which it is extraordinarily pleasant to wander. Stop at the central **bazaar,** which is a busy marketplace where cobblers and metalsmiths ply their trades. Tall minarets mark the city's mosques; note especially **Saatli Cami** (formerly Agios Ioannis), named after its clocktower. Just north and up a hill is the Taxiarchis Church, soon to open as a museum.

The best beaches are a few miles south of the city at **Sarımsaklı.** While the center of the beach is quite developed, the edges are still relatively quiet. If you wish to go farther out to sea, boat excursions leave from Ayvalık (near the information booth on the waterfront) every morning; the trip lasts for most of the day, includes the nearby islands, and makes frequent swimming stops.

Pergamum

When the pleasures of the modern world begin to seem too familiar, head to Pergamum, 54 km (33 miles) south of Ayvalık on Route E87. Pergamum was once the royal city of the Attalids, and the most magnificent Hellenistic city in Asia Minor. While it's perfectly possible to race through ancient Pergamum in a morning, you will be rewarded if you decide to spend a day here, for this was one of the greatest and most beautiful of all Greek cities, and its ruins speak eloquently of its past.

The Attalid Dynasty

The city became famous in the third century B.C. when Lysimachus, a general in Alexander's army, deposited the considerable treasure he had accumulated during years of war behind its walls for safe-keeping. Sadly, he died in battle not long after, and his officer, Philetarus, inherited the lot. Philetarus set about founding a dynasty, adopting (he is said to have been a eunuch) a nephew, Eumenes, to succeed him. Under Eumenes and his descendants (variously named Attalus and Eumenes), the Attalid rulers of Pergamum became famous for defeating the invading Gauls, forming a military alliance with the Romans, and steadily increasing their wealth through war and exploitation of the surrounding silver mines and pasture land. By the time Attalus III bequeathed the city to the Romans, it was several hundred thousand strong, immense by the standards of the day.

The ruins are scattered across a fairly large area; it's best to start your visit at the Acropolis, on a rocky hill 6 km (4 miles) above the modern town of **Bergama,** and then explore the Asklepion near the town.

Parking is available outside the Royal Gate, and concession stands there sell site maps. Climb up to the **Temple of Trajan** near the summit; its Corinthian columns have been partially restored, and as you stand between them you'll have a lovely view of the surrounding countryside. Below is what's left of the Temple of Athena and the Altar of Zeus. The altar was raided by German "archaeologists" in the 19th century who sent back its magnificent frieze, depicting the battle between the gods and the giants, to Berlin's Pergamon Museum, along with a collection of other art from the site; only its enormous slab remains. The Temple, dating to the third century B.C., housed Pergamum's famous library. Founded by Attalus II, it once housed 200,000 volumes, partly written on papyrus and partly on bound parchment, which the scribes began to use when Egypt, fearing that the library here would outshine the one at Alexandria, banned the export of papyrus to Pergamum. The library was a magnet

Visitors stroll through the Roman ruins of Asklepieion in Pergamum, long ago an important center of medicine.

for scholars and historians until the fourth century A.D. Just offstage is the Temple of Dionysos.

A staircase leads down to the **theater.** Beautifully preserved, its 80 rows of seats could accommodate 10,000. Performances took place on a removable wooden stage (you can still see holes for the supporting posts). You might want to test the theater's superb acoustics; as in most ancient arenas, a conversationally pitched voice can be heard clearly from the highest seats.

The Asklepieion

The Asklepieion is situated well below the Acropolis, within walking distance of Bergama. Built in the second century A.D. under the Romans, it was a center of ancient medicine — Galen, perhaps the world's first anatomist and physiologist, trained here before he joined the court of Marcus Aurelius in Rome. Ancient medicine was systematic, but had striking differences from the way medicine is practiced today — the patient would sleep in the temple and dream, the physician would interpret the dream, and treatment, be it fasting or sacrifice to the gods or certain exercise, would be prescribed accordingly. A great deal of private contemplation was also involved, as the site's open spaces, originally colonnaded, attest to. Remnants of the original **Temple of Asklepios** library (a branch of the Great Library on the Acropolis), sacred fountain, and theater still stand.

İzmir

Turkey's second largest port, İzmir, 80 km (48 miles) south of Bergama on the coast road, is nearly impossible to avoid on a trek down the Aegean Coast. This isn't all bad — while İzmir is the gritty industrial center of the region, it has its own interests. First, the city claims to be the birthplace of Homer. And second, Alexander the Great (who left his mark throughout the region) had a dream that inspired his generals to build a fortified settlement here in the fourth century B.C. They did, the city prospered under the Romans, suffered under Arab invasions, and enjoyed a long period of prosperity as part of the Byzantine empire, most notably as a key stop on the Silk Route from Asia. But then, after the defeat of the Ottoman empire at the end of World War I, İzmir (which had always had a large Greek population) was occupied by the Greek army, who had been given a mandate over the region by the Allies. The Greeks moved a huge force to the city and began to press inland, infuriating nationalist resistance fighters under the command of Kemal Atatürk. In September 1922, the Turks drove the Greeks off of the mainland. The fighting and atrocities in İzmir were intense: Almost 70% of the city burned to the ground, thousands of civilians died, and a quarter-million non-Muslim residents were summarily expelled. Most refugees went to Greece (where İzmir is known as

Smyrna, and İstanbul as Constantinople), and they fueled a deep and abiding hatred and distrust between the Turks and the Greeks that affects international politics to this day.

The current incarnation of İzmir is built on these ruins. With its wide, tree-lined boulevards and characterless buildings, it has the feel of a city of the 1920s. The harbor is beautiful, best appreciated from the walls of the **Kadifekale** (Velvet Fortress), first built in Alexander's time and since restored. Leave the fortress through the main gate via the road to the left; you'll see stone steps on the right that lead to the agora, the original Roman market at the bottom of the hill. Continue strolling towards Konak Square on the sea, which marks the beginning of İzmir's outdoor bazaar. The city is best known for its leather products. Several streets to the south, on Bahribaba Park, is the city's very good **archaeological museum,** which holds statues excavated from the agora, as well as other statues, tombs, and friezes from the area.

Çeşme

Just 81 km (50 miles) west of İzmir on Route 300, is Çeşme, one of the coast's most charming resorts. Resort may be overstating things: This is really a sleepy little town, crowned by a Genoese castle, and surrounded by some of the best swimming beaches on the Aegean Coast. Pirlanta beach to the south, and Ilica beach to the east, are two of the nicest.

Sardis

The ancient city of Sardis, 90 km (55 miles) east of İzmir on Route 300, lies near the junction of the roads from Ephesus, Smyrna, Pergamum, and inner Asia Minor — a strategic position that made it, for centuries, the chief city of Asia Minor. The surrounding mountains are rich in gold ore, and coins were first minted here; the city's last Lydian ruler,

King Croesus (sixth century B.C.) was famous for his wealth and power — his hegemony extended over most of the cities on the Aegean. Cyrus the Great, leader of the Persians, took notice, and Croesus, unsure if he should attack first or wait to be attacked, consulted the oracle at Delphi. With characteristic ambiguity, the oracle replied that if Croesus attacked he would destroy a great empire. Croesus did attack, and the empire destroyed was his own.

Cyrus used Sardis as the political and military base for his conquest of Asia Minor and his assaults on Greece. Like the rest of the region, Sardis passed from ruler to ruler over the next centuries. In A.D. 17 an earthquake destroyed it; what remains are ruins of the Roman rebuilding of this fabled city.

The ruins are spread over a large area. The huge **Temple of Artemis** is near the parking lot. Begun in the fourth century B.C., it was never finished, although construction continued for more than 400 years. Eventually, its stones were looted for use in other buildings. It now consists of a huge foundation with a few Roman columns scattered about. It's worthwhile to make a circuit of its grounds, however, for the setting of the Temple — amidst forested hills and angular rock pinnacles — is very beautiful. About a kilometer (half a mile) to the northeast is a **gymnasium** built in the third century A.D.; its Marble Court has been beautifully restored. A nearby **synagogue** was probably given to the local Jewish community by a Roman emperor in the second century A.D.; it has been restored and offers a picture of Jewish worship not long past the lifetime of Christ.

☞ Ephesus

The gleaming marble monuments of Ephesus, 79 km (49 miles) south of İzmir on the coast road, comprise one of the best-preserved ancient cities on the Mediterranean, and are an absolute magnet for tourists. While you shouldn't miss Ephesus, it would serve you well to plan your trip carefully — arrive early (the site opens at 8am), map out your route (you might wish to invest in a site map), and bring water, as the acres of lovely stone here get very hot as the sun rises. Note that Ephesus and the adjacent village of Selçuk are really a pair — what you see in the Selçuk museum will illuminate your visit to the ancient city, and Selçuk is the site of the great Temple of Artemis, which was one of the seven wonders of the ancient world.

Set on a sheltered harbor and at the mouth of a river, Ephesus has been a settlement for millennia. It was originally built by immigrant Athenians in 1000 B.C., was conquered by the rich King Croesus (who moved the city a bit closer to the sea), and was then held, in relatively peaceful succession, by the Persians, Alexander, the Romans, and the Byzantines. Originally founded to celebrate the Greek goddess Artemis, the city moved as smoothly through its various religious

In the theater of Ephesus actors and chorus performed the great works of Classical drama.

incarnations as it did through its political ones. Both Saint Paul and Saint John the Evangelist preached here (Saint John may have been accompanied by the elderly Mary), and the city was the site of two church councils. The decline of the worship of Artemis somehow sapped Ephesus of its founders' vigor; this, and the silting of its harbor caused it to decline in both influence and size during the Byzantine era.

Nonetheless, what remains is magnificent; what follows is a brief suggested itinerary. Leave the parking lot via a road that passes the first century A.D. **stadium.** Designed to seat 70,000, the stadium was a venue for everything from chariot races to gladiatorial contests. A well-preserved monumental gate on the west side was the principle entrance. Double back through the car park then make your way to the Theater. Started in the Hellenistic period (and heavily restored in the current period), what stands today is almost entirely Roman. It is a huge semicircle backed by Mount Pion;

> Since it is improper for Turkish men and women who are unacquainted to sit together on a bus, expect the driver to make some last-minute seating arrangements.

notice that the pitch increases as you climb up the rows of seats, allowing a clear view of the stage for spectators in the upper reaches. The theater could seat 24,000 and, over the centuries, viewers were treated to plays, as well as the preaching of Saint Paul; in modern times the theater hosts music and dance performances in May.

The Theater stands at one end of the **Arcadian Way,** a wide colonnaded street that runs to the middle harbor gate. Built in the fifth century A.D., it was the model of an urban thoroughfare. On either side were covered walkways lined with shops. The walkways protected strollers from the sun and the rain, and were illuminated at night with lamps.

Crews from ships made their way into the city by the Way, and they must have mingled with the townspeople here, exchanging news of the outside world while they relaxed in this comfortable, cosmopolitan place.

Walk back to the Theater and follow Marble Avenue, paved with marble slabs, to the Library of Celsus. This is another structure that has been extensively restored. It was erected in the second century A.D. by the Roman Consul Gaius Julius Aquila, who was subsequently buried in an ornate sarcophagus under the building's western wall, where he still lies. The library housed 12,000 scrolls that were stored in niches separated from the outer walls, to protect them from heat and humidity. It was excavated and restored by Austrian archaeologists (who carried its ornamental reliefs to a museum in Vienna).

Near the library, the Street of Kuretes crosses the Marble Avenue, and at the corner is the city's brothel. Rooms surround a central atrium and, in the main reception room, a mosaic depicting the four seasons covers the floor — winter and autumn are best preserved. The small **Temple of Hadrian** lies farther down the street. Dedicated in the second century A.D. as a gift to the city and to Artemis, this gracious structure, fronted by Corinthian columns, has been restored; the friezes you see are plaster and the originals are in the museum in Selçuk. On the far side of the street, note another large mosaic that presumably fronted a row of shops. Behind it, steps lead up to the **terrace houses.** These airy, frescoed, mosaic-decorated structures were home to citizens of Ephesus in the Imperial and early Byzantine period. If open to visitors (they are often closed to protect the delicate artwork within), they will give you an idea of what life was like for the well-to-do.

The Street of Kuretes continues past the Odeon, a small theater for poetry readings and music, to the Magnesian

Gate. A colonnaded road to the Temple of Artemis begins here; also, caravans bound for the east left from this point.

Selçuk

The living town attached to Ephesus, Selçuk began its rise to prominence in the fifth century A.D., when the harbor at Ephesus silted over. It has strong Christian associations: Saint John the Evangelist died here in about A.D. 100, and is buried on **Ayasoluk Hill,** which is a good spot to begin your tour. Several hundred years after John's death, the Emperor Justinian constructed an ornate Basilica here. Until its destruction in the 15th century by the Mongols, it was one of the largest in the world. Today, the church has been restored with funds, in part, from a church group in Lima, Ohio. A castle sits atop Ayasoluk Hill; its ramparts provide a wonderful view.

A quick scramble down the hill from the castle will bring you to the **archaeological museum,** which houses a really wonderful collection, mostly of artifacts from Ephesus. The first room holds smaller objects — a bronze of Eros riding a dolphin, miniatures from the Terrace Houses, a fine wall painting of Socrates, as well as a reconstruction of a room from the terrace houses. In Room 2, don't miss the statue of a young Dionysos, which once stood in Ephesus. Room 3 contains a collection of early crosses, and various representations of the Virgin and the saints. Some fine sarcophagi decorate the courtyard, and Room 4 continues this theme, displaying objects found in tombs. Room 5 is dedicated to Artemis, with several statues of the Goddess. Room 6 holds the frieze from Hadrian's Temple.

Just outside of town near the road to Ephesus, is the **Temple of Artemis.** It's hard to imagine how a former wonder of the ancient world could be a less impressive sight, but centuries of neglect and looting have taken their toll. Let your creativity reign, however, and you may be able to re-erect the 127 marble columns, re-create the magnificent friezes, and imagine the goddess of the hunt at home, and at rest. Another outlying place of interest is **Meryemana,** the House of the Virgin Mary, on the road from Ephesus to Bulbuldagi. Lore has it that Saint John and the Virgin lived in this simple dwelling after the death of Christ. Unsubstantiated as the claim is, Meryemana is usually thronged with pilgrims.

Don't be fooled by the name Ladies' Beach — both men and women are welcome to laze beneath the parasols.

Kuşadası

Nearby Kuşadası, 20 km (12 miles) southwest of Selçuk on Route 515, is a port for ferries and tour boats, and, as such, has become a jumping off point for group tours to Ephesus. It's a busy place, with some good restaurants and hotels, and a large bus station offering connections to most of the country. The small old center is atmospheric, and some really fine beaches are nearby. To the south, Kadinlar Denizi, "the ladies' beach," offers swimming to both sexes. A few miles to the north is Tusan beach, just off the coast road; another few miles along is Pamucak beach which, if the wind isn't too strong, has some of the best swimming in the area.

Pamukkale

From Kuşadası, Route E87 turns east into Turkey's interior, and the striking scenery and ruins at Pamukkale. It's a bit of a trek — 170 km (105 miles); look for signs after you pass Saraykoy — but is well worth the effort.

You'll see Pamukkale in the distance, a tall, chalky outcrop rising high above the surrounding plain. Come closer and the rocks will resolve into fantastic shapes resembling flowers, birds, waterfalls — there really is no limit to the forms they take: The source of this strange beauty is a spring that burbles up from the top of the plateau, putting out a stream of warm, calcium-rich water that, as it dribbles over the side and cools, precipitates into the hard white chalk called travertine. This has been occurring for millennia, creating an ever-changing phantasmagoria.

Swim among the artifacts scattered in the spring waters at Pamukkale.

The ancient city was called Hierapolis and may have been founded by Eumenes II of Pergamum. It was a favored city under the Romans, and became prosperous from trade in wool and an unusual marble colored by the seepage of minerals. It was also a spa and the waters were said to cure rheumatism. A large Jewish community laid the foundations for the growth of Christianity, and there were once hundreds of churches (some of which still stand) here. The city suffered under Arab attacks, and was virtually abandoned by the 12th century when it passed into Turkish hands. Italian archaeologists began excavations in the mid-20th century; the ensuing tourist development has, sadly, besmirched this once pristine site.

Access is from **Pamukkale Koyu,** a village at the base of the plateau. You can drive or hike up; try to enter via the North Gate. From here, it's almost irresistible to climb down onto the **travertine terraces** first. Pools of milky water are everywhere, and tourist authorities ask that you remove your shoes before stepping in. Note that for a proper bath in the curative waters you must visit the Pamukkale Hotel, on the plateau, where the once sacred pool, surrounded by gardens and a few fallen columns, is accessible for a fee.

Once cured, step out into the largely Roman ruins. A narrow road leads past the fourth century A.D. nymphaeum, or fountainhouse, to the Temple of Apollo. Started in the Hellenistic period and probably completed in the third century A.D., it is set on a shelf of natural rock. Not much remains of it. While excavating the temple foundation, Italian archaeologists were considerably troubled by noxious sulfur gas that

These mysteriously serene plateaus are the calcified waterfalls found at Pamukkale.

seemed to seep out of the rock. They found its source in the Plutonium just next door. This sanctuary, dedicated to Pluto, is set over a stream that runs through a deep, natural cutting in the rock. Gas, which certainly includes sulfurous compounds, rises from the water. It is deadly; only eunuchs, according to ancient writers, were immune to its toxicity. Farther along is a restored Roman theater. Many of the stage buildings have been preserved and, in June, this is the venue for an international song festival. Farther east, past the city walls, is the Martyrion of Saint Philip, a fifth-century structure built to honor his death here.

If you continue along the hillside, past the site of a theater, then down a hill to a picnic area, you'll see some huge arches on the right — these were originally Roman baths, but were later converted into a church. Just past them is the ancient city's **necropolis,** probably the largest cemetery in Asia Minor. For sanitary reasons, burial was not permitted inside the city proper, and the tombs here date back to the Hellenistic period. They were surrounded with gardens, and special guilds were entrusted with tending the tombs, some of which are elaborately designed and inscribed. Retrace your steps to the baths; a short distance past them is a great colonnaded street. Once the commercial center of the city, it is now traversed by sun-worshipping lizards whose feet scratch lazily over the fallen marble.

> Tired? Try asking *Yakinda otel var mi?* (Is there a hotel nearby?)

Aphrodisias

On your way back to the coast, turn south off E87 onto Route 585, which will take you to Aphrodisias, 80 km (50 miles) from Pamukkale. Named for the Greek goddess of love, the city was a cultural and not a commercial center, known for its school of sculpture and devotion to the cult of Aphrodite. The carefully excavated ruins that remain, built mostly from the local blue-veined marble, give the city an other-worldly air.

Route 585 follows the course of the Maeander River through fertile, green countryside to the lofty site of the ancient city. Set on a 600-m-(1,900-ft-) high plateau, and ringed with craggy, marble-veined mountains, it is a strikingly beautiful place. The ruins, most of which date to the first and second centuries A.D., were obscured by the village of Geyre until 1956 when an earthquake struck. The villagers were relocated a mile to the west, and excavations have revealed an entire ancient city on par with Ephesus. Note that the ongoing digging means that some monuments will be closed to visitors.

Note the intricate detail, still very much apparent in this ornately carved Roman Sarcophagus.

A path loops around the site. The first-century **theater** is beautifully preserved; behind the stage is a large square, or tetrastoon, where Roman and Byzantine citizens might have congregated after a performance. Follow the path past the north flank of the theater; below is the **Sebasteion.** This first century complex, consisting of twin porticos and a central paved area, was probably first constructed as a shrine to Aphrodite, and later became a place to honor the Roman emperors. Making an emperor divine and equal to the ancient gods was a way to legitimize Roman hegemony in the east, and the Sebasteion served this purpose. A double agora is nearby, its blue-gray marble columns almost indistinguishable from the surrounding poplar trees. Beyond it are the well-preserved Baths of Hadrian.

To the north is the so-called Bishop's Palace, which probably began life as the Roman governor's residence. Next are the remains of the **Temple of Aphrodite.** Construction here probably started in the first century B.C. By the fifth century A.D. the temple was converted into a Christian basilica and the great statue of the goddess of love that stood here was largely destroyed; her battered torso was incorporated into a Byzantine-era wall. Just north is the school of philosophy.

Perhaps the finest structure in Aphrodisias is the **stadium,** the best preserved in all of Anatolia. Built in the first century A.D. and designed to seat 30,000 spectators, the competitions staged here were a copy of those played at Delphi's Pythian Games — foot racing, boxing, and wrestling, as well as music, oratory, and drama. Prizes were modest, and contestants entered simply for the privilege of competition, a decidedly non-modern idea that is one of the most inspiring legacies of the ancient world. Just doing something well, the ancients tell us, is its own reward.

Finish your visit in the **museum,** which offers a well-organized display of statuary from the site.

Priene

Back on the coast, some 37 km (23 miles) from Kuşadası, Priene is an ancient Ionian city in an exquisite setting of pine-clad terraces on the flank of Samsun Daği. It was probably first settled by Greeks in the 11th century B.C. The city whose ruins remain today was laid out in the fourth century B.C. on a grid system. As the harbor silted over, the wealth of Priene declined, invaders lost interest, and so it remains an almost purely Hellenistic city, one of the few on the Aegean coast.

The ruins are a steep clamber up from the parking lot. Although they are well-marked, it's useful to take a look at a site map first. Main streets run east-west and are intersected by smaller lanes, creating "insula" which contain either four private houses or the city's public and religious buildings. Note the drainage gutters on the sides of the streets, and the grooves in the center, which were worn by chariot wheels. Just left of the main street is the second-century B.C. *bouleuterion,* or council house. Rows of seats on three sides enclose a small square, and a speaker's recess, where speakers stood to address the council, is on the fourth. The building would have been covered by a wooden roof. Just across the street are the scanty remains of the sacred stoa, the agora, and the Temple of Zeus, which formed the heart of the city. Farther along the main street is a largely residential section of thick-walled houses, designed so that rooms opened off of a central courtyard.

Two terraces above the main street is the **Temple of Athena Polias.** Built in part with contributions from Alexander the Great, it is one of the most harmoniously designed temples on the Aegean Coast and served as a model for students of architecture for centuries; five of the original 30 Ionic columns have been re-erected. Note the fourth-century B.C. theater, another terrace up. Finally, if it's not too hot and you are

Standing tall — the Ionian columns remain erect at the Temple of Athena in the Hellenistic city of Priene.

feeling exceptionally energetic, climb to the top of the Acropolis. It will take you more than one hour, but the view of Priene, the green valley of the Maeander River, and the sea in the distance is magnificent.

Didyma

Just 36 km (22 miles) south of Priene is Didyma, the site of a magnificent Temple of Apollo. If you've begun to suffer from Ionian relic overload, some fine swimming beaches are nearby.

There is a small town here now, composed primarily of souvenir shops and mediocre restaurants, but for most of its history Didyma was an oracle of Apollo. Its sacred precincts were home to a priestess who, after inhaling vapors from a spring, would go into a trance and answer the difficult questions about love, family, and ambition that plagued the ancients (as well as the moderns). An early shrine was destroyed by the Persians, and a new temple was planned when Alexander the Great retook the region. Its grand scale almost ensured that it would never be completed and, although work went on for some five centuries, it never was. What was done, however, is striking.

Try to visit at sunset, when the temple's columns glow in the darkening light. The temple was designed to be bounded by 108 columns in double rows (some of which have been re-erected), all set on an imposingly high crepidoma, or stepped platform. As you enter, you'll see a Roman Medusa head, one of the few original pieces of statuary left

Giris **(entrance) and** *cikis* **(exit).**

on the site. In a well below the head, pilgrims would purify themselves, then make their way to the temple shrine, where they would receive the oracle's answers. Further inside the temple is the foundation of the naiskos, the great hall that contained the cult statue and sacred spring.

There are some good swimming beaches near Didyma. **Altinkum,** about 5 km (3 miles) to the south, boasts a half-mile-long golden sand beach that is quite developed. A quieter beach to the north is at **Tavşanburnu.**

Bodrum

Facing south, and set on two curved bays, Bodrum, 125 km (78 miles) from Didyma, is one of Turkey's premier resorts. Because height limits for buildings have long been in effect, the blue Aegean is never long out of sight. There are a number of good restaurants in Bodrum and, in contrast to much of the Aegean coast, a fairly active nightlife scene.

Known in ancient times as Halikarnassos, the area was colonized by Greeks in the 11th century B.C., came to power as a more or less independent part of the Persian empire, and declined slowly after Alexander's armies passed through. In the 15th century, the crusading Knights of Saint John built a fine castle in Bodrum; in later centuries the peninsula was home to a largely ethnically Greek population and, although the Greeks were expelled in 1922, the area retains a vaguely Greek feel.

The boating set is drawn to the nightlife and magnificent beaches of Bodrum.

The modern town of Bodrum is crowned by the **castle of Saint Peter,** a heavily fortified structure that was, for years, the only Christian outpost in Anatolia. Many of the stones in the castle were salvaged from the famous Mausoleum of Halikarnassos, final resting place of the fourth-century B.C. ruler Mausoleus, and one of the seven wonders of the ancient world. Today, the castle is a multi-level maze of courtyards, rooms, museums, moats, and cisterns; there's even a dungeon. Don't miss the so-called Glass Wreck Hall, where a Byzantine ship and its cargo, circa 1025, are housed. Bodrum's bazaar is just north of the castle; the site of the ancient mausoleum is two blocks above the harbor, and is surrounded by a charming neighborhood of small stone houses. Little is left of the mausoleum itself.

A peninsula stretches out to the west of Bodrum, and while parts of it are no more than a thicket of high-rise hotels, some towns and beaches are quite lovely. Small boats at the harbor offer short cruises. There is also frequent bus service into the peninsula. On the south shore, **Bagla** has a fine sand beach, at **Karaincir** you can rent windsurfing boards, Akyarlar boasts some good restaurants, and **Gümüşlük** is a quiet village with another fine beach. On the north shore, **Gundogan,** with its reliable winds, is a local center for windsurfing and sailing.

MEDITERRANEAN COAST

The southern coast of Turkey takes on many names, among them the "Turquoise Coast" and the "Turkish Riviera." While these labels felicitously suggest long sandy strands, crystal-clear waters, and pleasant resorts, this craggy landscape also cradles the evocative ruins of past civilizations, centuries-old cities and spectacular mountain scenery.

Marmaris and the Datça Peninsula

The first settlement of any size along the Mediterranean coast is a brash, boisterous resort town and yacht port whose saving grace is the presence of a fleet of boats ensuring an easy getaway to more pleasant places. Aside from a seemingly endless line of harborside drinking establishments, the allure of Marmaris is its beautiful setting on a bay framed on one side by the Datça Peninsula and backed by forests; several beaches (the closest and most accessible are İçmeler Beach and the strand in Günlünçek National Park); and the small, white-washed old town. An exploration of the narrow lanes begins at the spice-filled bazaar and ends at the **castle,** built in 1522 during an Ottoman campaign against nearby Rhodes. The courtyard garden here is the most restful spot

Traditional Turkish gulets line the harbor at Marmaris, ready to take passengers along the coast.

in town, and the views of sea and coastline from the ramparts are stunning.

Datça, at the end of the peninsula of the same name, retains the air of a fishing village. If you are seeking quiet seclusion, Datça well rewards the two-hour drive along the steep, twisting dirt track that rises and falls through dense pine forests and clings to cliffs high above secluded coves.

Datça is only a short boat ride away from **Knidos,** a seventh-century B.C. Dorian Greek settlement majestically poised on a windswept headland commanding the juncture of the Aegean and the Mediterranean seas. This position on the major shipping lanes earned Knidos a prominent role in the ancient world. Aside from the rough-hewn beauty of the city's ruined temples, agora, theater and Byzantine church, as well as some curiosities such as the sundial used by the astronomer Eudoxus, Knidos seems to be most noted for what's no longer here. The city's famed lion tomb is now in the British Museum, as is a statue of goddess of Demeter, both unearthed by archaeologists in the 1850s. Most famous in antiquity was the long-lost, fourth-century B.C. statue of Aphrodite by Praxiteles. Pliny praised the sculpted nude as the finest statue in the world, and travelers sailed to Knidos from all over the ancient world to see it.

Dalyan

This relaxed town can be reached by boat from Marmaris, and it is only 75 km (46 miles) east along the coast road, Route 400. The tree-shaded village center stretches beneath a cliff laced with the fourth-century B.C. rock tombs of the Carian civilization and alongside a slow-moving, reed-lined river, the Dalyan Cayı. Pleasant as these environs are, a visitor won't be in town too long before boarding a boat and embarking on some extraordinary excursions. A short way upstream the river opens into **Lake Köyceğiz,** an inland sea lined with woods that shelter

The bounty available for sale at the bazaar in Datça is proof positive of the freshness of Mediterranean cuisine.

kingfishers, herons, storks, and other birds. Boatmen usually ferry their passengers first to Köyceğiz, a sleepy lakeside fishing village, then cross the lake to the **Sultaniye thermal springs;** the facilities are a bit worn, but a soak in the warm, mineral rich waters is quite soothing.

About half a mile downstream from Dalyan, boats pull ashore at the ruins of the city of **Kaunos,** famous in antiquity for figs and malaria. Settled in the ninth-century B.C. by the Carians, the city much later passed through Greek and Roman hands and was closely allied with the Lycian civilization farther east along the coast. This mixed heritage accounts for the presence of Roman baths, a Greek-style theater, and Lycian-type rock tombs, with elaborate façades that suggest the entrances to palatial residences. Some of the most impressive remnants to emerge from the jungle-like undergrowth are the extensive walls, the oldest parts of which date to the fourth century B.C.

Downstream, the river winds through tall reeds then emerges at **İstuzu Beach.** Aside from some makeshift concessions, this unbroken stretch of sand, 8 km (5 miles) long, is blessedly devoid of manmade incursions, protected as it is a breeding ground of the loggerhead turtle *(Caretta*

History-hungry tourists step carefully down the seats of the Roman theater at Kaunos.

caretta). You're likely to see the creatures' tracks, but not the turtles themselves, as the beach is off-limits at night from May to October when the females lumber ashore to nest and the hatchlings scurry into the sea.

Fethiye

This busy farming town, 90 km (55 miles) east of Dalyan along Route 400, is more concerned with the here and now than with the ancient past. It's not that Fethiye doesn't have a very long history, for the city was founded in the fifth century B.C. as Telmessos and was ruled by the various civilizations that subdued this coastline over the centuries. The town has changed its name several times accordingly, to Anastasiopolis and Megri under the Byzantines to Fethiye in the 1930s, in honor of a local war hero.

Earthquakes, the most recent in 1957, have laid waste to most remnants of this past. Even so, a few Lycian-style tombs are scattered about the dusty streets and cut into the cliffs that frame the southern edge of town; the fragments of an ancient theater have recently been excavated; a crusader castle tops a hilltop; and the town museum is richly endowed with local archaeo-logical finds. Most likely to capture your attention are the produce stands, bazaar, and the general air of an

> **BYOT** — That's "Bring your own tissue," because it is often not available in public restrooms.

ordinary, workaday Turkish town. Fethiye is especially appealing in the evening, when what seems to be the entire population turns out to stroll alongside the harbor promenades. By day, boats depart from here for the hidden coves and isolated beaches of the **Twelve Islands and Gemile Island,** where Lycian and Byzantine ruins are scattered across the mountainsides.

An enticing network of roads, many no more than dusty tracks, traverses the dusty landscape around Fethiye, north to the popular beach at Çalış and south to the more pleasant, quieter strand at Gemiler. The town of Kaya Köyü, 7 km (4.5 miles) along a narrow lane from Fethiye's castle, is a recent ruin, rendered so during the population exchanges of 1923 following the Greek-Turkish war. The town's 400 or so small houses and its two basilicas have been abandoned since their Christian inhabitants of Greek descent sailed back to Greece from the docks in Fethiye.

Ölüdeniz

Turkey's most famous beach, 15 km (9 miles) south of Fethiye, is much touted on travel posters, and can be quite crowded. Even so, the warm waters of the Ölüdeniz lagoon,

The picture-perfect beaches at Ölüdeniz draw visitors for obvious reasons — beware of large crowds!

backed by white beaches and hillsides scented with pines, are delightful nonetheless. To enjoy this lovely coast in quieter surroundings, seek out the beach at Kidrak, 3 km (2 miles) east, or make the short crossing to Saint Nicholas Island.

The Ruins of the Lycian Heartland

The tall coastal mountains and fertile valleys east and south of Fethiye and Ölüdeniz cradled the Lycian civilization. Establishing themselves here in the seventh century B.C., the Lycians formed a democratic union known as the Lycian Federation that continued to function even as they lost their independence to successive conquerors that included the Persians, Greeks, Alexander the Great, Rhodians and eventually Imperial Rome. The Lycians left behind bountiful traces of their presence here, from their coinage, among the world's first, to their rock tombs, and most notably, their ruined cities that can be reached with relative ease from turnoffs along Route 400.

Tlos and Pinara

The ruins of Tlos and Pinara crown hilltops on opposite sides of the valley of the Xanthos river, now known as the Eşen Cayı. At **Tlos,** 22 km (14 miles) east of Fethiye, the most extensive ruins from the city's lengthy past are its seventh-century B.C. rock tombs and the Roman theater and baths. The carvings here are unusually rich; the most elaborate of the many tombs bears depictions of the mythical Bellerophon riding the winged horse Pegasus, and fragments of the theater are decorated with actors' masks. Of more recent vintage is the 18th-century fortress, dramatically perched above the rest of the town and the valley with the peaks of the Akdağ range in the background. The castle, the lair of the 19th-century pirate Kanlı Ali Ağa, affords a tantalizing glimpse of the nearby **Saklikent gorge.** A narrow road leads to the mouth of this narrow chasm, accessible only by a path that follows the base of a sheer, towering rock face past rushing rapids and cascades deep into the silent mountains.

Pinara, across the valley and 20 km (12 miles) south of Tlos, is less accessible than its neighbor. A half-hour climb from the village of Minare may well provide you with the somewhat eerie experience of finding yourself alone among lonely ruins scattered among olive trees at the base of a massive cliff honey-combed with tombs. Richly carved tombs are also among the best-preserved structures in the town below; the so-called Royal Tomb is especially decorative, covered with depictions of cityscapes and scenes of what appears to be a religious festival. The Greek theater, rising above copses and olive trees, is exquisite — small, perfectly proportioned, and elegant, with its stage house still intact.

The Letoön

The Letoön, 16 km (10 miles) south of Pinara, is not a city but a religious sanctuary, a shrine to the goddess Leto and an assembly ground to which Lycians traveled from their various cities to celebrate festivals. Greek legend had it that Leto was a nymph who had the misfortune of enchanting Zeus, a situation that invoked the wrath of his jealous wife, Hera. Pregnant and in flight from Hera's revenge, Leto befriended wolves who led her to the Xanthos river to refresh herself; the incident allegedly gave the culture we call Lycian its name, a derivation of the Greek *lykos,* for wolf. Leto was not without a vengeful side of her own — she turned two local shepherds who refused her water into frogs.

The first of the **three temples,** dating to the third century B.C., is dedicated to Leto, and the other two to the twins she bore here in the Xanthos valley, Artemis and Apollo. The

The Temple of Leto is one of three ancient temples at the major Lycian religious sanctuary, the Letoön.

center temple is believed to have been dedicated to Artemis and the third to Apollo; a mosaic on the floor of the Apollo temple symbolically depicts both twins, with a bow and quiver for Artemis and a lyre for Apollo. In the nymphaeum, the large pool is surrounded by empty niches from which the statuary has long since vanished, a fate that has also befallen the masks that once adorned the otherwise well-preserved Greek theater.

Xanthos

Xanthos, directly across the valley from the Letoön, is the most important of the Lycian cities and its ruins the most extensive. Anyone who's read *The Iliad* may well remember the mythical character Glaucus "from the whirling waters of Xanthos." The city's most noted associations are

Much of the rich culture of Patara is still buried beneath the sand but some ruins — like this tomb — are visible.

with independence and tragedy. Rather than succumb to conquerors, the residents of Xanthos twice set their city and themselves ablaze, once during an onslaught by the Persian general Harpagus in 540 B.C., and again when the Roman general Brutus laid siege to the city in 42 B.C.

Like the other Lycian cities, Xanthos is littered with **rock tombs,** including a fifth-century B.C. pillar tomb inscribed with 250 lines describing the exploits of local soldiers in the Peloponesian Wars; this is the most extensive known script in the Lycian language. The so-called Tomb of the Harpies is also richly carved with figures that are half man and half bird and appear to be ushering the dead into the afterlife. These reliefs are not the originals — they and many other monumental artifacts were carried away from Xanthos in 1842 by archaeologist Charles Fellows. Some, including the Ionic temple known as the Nereid Monument, are now in the British Museum in London. Of the monuments that remain in Xanthos, the city gate and theater are Roman in style, and a monastery and a basilica with extensive mosaics are Byzantine.

Patara

The principal port of Lydia and a sophisticated urban center in antiquity, Patara is 18 km (11 miles) south of Xanthos. The oracle of Apollo resided here, in a temple that is still lost beneath the sands, and Hannibal and Saint Paul were among the city's many noted visitors. Saint Nicholas, the son of a wealthy trader, was born in Patara in A.D. 270. Today, Patara is romantically half buried beneath constantly shifting sand dunes that appear to be on the brink of obliterating all traces of the baths complex, theater, gateway, and other buildings and monuments of the once thriving city.

The presence of these ruins, and the prospect of many more to be uncovered, accounts in part for the other great attraction in Patara — a 15-km (9-mile) long **beach** that is all but deserted, despite its lovely sands washed by warm surf. This solitude makes the beach a haven for nudists as well as loggerhead turtles, who nest here between May and October. Gelemiş, a ramshackle village at a crossroads on the 6-km (4-mile) road leading from Route 400 to the ruins and the beach, offers basic amenities.

Kalkan

This pleasant seaside town and its neighbor down the coast, Kaş, are relatively free of important ruins. Instead, they provide the sight-weary traveler with such pleasures as bougainvillea-shaded café terraces and breezy seaside promenades. Both are excellent bases from which to explore the coast.

Kalkan, 13 km (8 miles) east of the Patara turnoff on Route 400, is the smaller of the two towns. Stone, tile-roofed houses, some occupied by shops, restaurants, and *pansiyons,* cling to a steep hillside that drops to a small harbor. Although Kalkan is no longer the remote fishing and farming village it once was, it retains a quiet, pleasant atmosphere and is especially popular with Turkish vacationers. What Kalkan doesn't have is a sandy beach, and swimmers instead content themselves with a small pebble strand and diving platforms that float in the harbor. Those in need of a real beach make the 6-km (4-mile) trip east along the coast to **Kapautaş,** a much-discovered hideaway reached from narrow steps off the roadside and at the head of a deep gorge of the same name.

☞ Kaş

This once sleepy timber-shipping port, 30 km (18 miles) east of Kalkan on Route 400, was known in antiquity as Aspendos and as Andifli until the early years of the 20th century. Kaş is now quite lively but retains an easy-going air, and the setting, along a curving bay beneath limestone cliffs and pine-covered mountains, is lovely. The shady streets are lined with small houses and the occasional rock tomb or two, and a small, intact Greek-style theater graces a seaside olive grove a short walk to the west of the mosque at the town center.

Kaş is a popular port of call for gulet trips along the coast, and the harbor is also filled with excursion boats that set out for nearby islands. One of these islands is **Kastellorizon,** the farthest flung of the Greek Dodecanese and only a few miles off the coast. Visitors making the trip from Kaş are officially allowed to remain on the island only a day, though this is plenty of time to explore the port, crusader castle, and unblemished countryside.

☞ Kekova

Many boats set sail for Kekova Island, which gives its name to a beautiful and fascinating coastline just east of Kaş. You can also drive into the region, following a narrow road that leads off

Route 400 toward the village of Ucagiz from a turnoff about 20 km (12 miles) east of Kaş. Little fishing villages overlook placid lagoons, and the sea bed beneath the warm waters is littered with Greek columns, the foundations of Roman houses, and Lycian tombs.

Üçağiz is the larger of the two settlements of any size in Kekova. The village is still quite rustic, and though its residents continue to make their living from fishing, they are willing to forsake their lines and nets to ferry passengers along the coast. The usual destination is the north coast of **Kekova Island,** where the underwater ruins are known as the Sunken City; a ruined Byzantine basilica forms a picturesque backdrop to a pop-

The tiny fishing port at Kale on Kekova Island is as quaint a Mediterranean village as you will find anywhere.

ular spot for swimming, though the waters around the island are officially off limits because of the presence of so many submerged antiquities.

Kale is a terribly picturesque village that is huddled beneath a castle built by the Knights of Saint John returning from the crusades. The scramble up the narrow path to the ramparts rewards you with sweeping views and a look at a theater carved into the side of the cliff. Down below, the little harbor is studded with half-submerged Lycian tombs. The incongruous presence of a helicopter landing pad can be attributed to wealthy Turkish businessman Rahmi Koç, who retreats to a simple house in the village and has endowed a local school and other institutions.

Demre (Kale)

Another Kale is just down the coast, about 35 km (21 miles) east of Kaş. This Kale is also known as Demre, and despite this confusing nomenclature, the town is best and most simply known for the presence of Saint Nicholas, the fourth-century B.C. bishop of the nearby ancient city of Myra.

Though the saint's remains have long since been removed to the church of San Nicola in Bari, Italy, Demre's **basilica of Saint Nicholas** has commemorated the saint, whose legendary generosity seems to have originated from his practice

Statues of St. Nicholas in all shapes and sizes are commonplace in Kale.

of giving coins to poor households by anonymously dropping them down the chimney, since the fifth century. The odd pillar or two and other remains of the original church are difficult to locate among subsequent alterations, including 19th-century renovations that added a belfry and vaulted ceiling over the nave and were sponsored by Tsar Nicholas I of Russia (Nicholas is Russia's patron saint.)

A walk or drive north of the town center, along dusty roads lined with greenhouses sheltering the tomatoes and citrus fruits that are the town's mainstay, brings you to **Myra.** This riverside city was an important center of Lycian commerce, as evidenced by its impressive monuments — most notably, a well-preserved theater with 35 rows of seats from which spectators enjoyed the spectacle of gladiators fighting off wild beasts trapped in the nearby mountains. Most of the tombs here are clustered in the so-called Riverside Necropolis and the Sea Necropolis, and some charmingly duplicate rather humble wood-beamed Lycian dwellings.

From Demre to Antalya

From Kale, Route 400 follows the craggy coastline for about 30 km (18 miles) and comes to Finike, a sleepy agricultural town. A short detour north from here for about 32 km (20 miles) brings you to the ruins of **Arykanda,** which cling picturesquely to pine-covered hillsides on either side of a gorge. Tombs, the Roman marketplace, and

> A conversation opener:
> *Ingilizce biliyor musunuz?*
> **(Do you speak English?)**

several ancient streets are scattered beneath the trees. In the well-preserved Roman baths complex, walls, window frames, and mosaic flooring are still intact. The coast road brings you in short order to two more ancient sites, beautifully located beside the sea.

Olympos

The ruins of warehouses, villas, and other structures of this long-abandoned port city, about 35 km (22 miles) east of Finike, stretch along the banks of a tree-shaded stream that, in the shadow of two Byzantine forts, courses across the wide sands to the sea. While the ruins here are a bit scanty, at least for this part of the world, the experience of walking through the stony fragments to a chorus of birdsong then swimming from the pine-backed beach is memorable. Olympos is also the name of the mountain that rises behind the ruins (one of many summits to bear the name in the ancient world) and a steep, dusty climb of at least an hour up its flanks brings you to the **Sanctuary of Hephaistos.** A vent of natural gas here continues to issue a flame, as it was doing millennia ago when sailors on Roman trading ships recorded a natural beacon along this part of the coast. It was on the summit of Olympos that the mythical character Bellerophon is said to have defeated the dragon-like Chimera.

Phaselis

Phaselis, 25 km (15 miles) east of Olympos, is a former colony of Rhodes and a strategically placed trading post with mercantile ties that stretched across the Mediterranean from Rome to Asia Minor. Phaselitans acquired quite a reputation in antiquity for being tight with money — in their case, with their distinctive coinage emblazoned with ships. In a trade reminiscent of the Dutch acquisition of the island of Manhattan for a string of beads, the seventh-century B.C. founders of the city are said to have purchased the territory for some dried fish. Their descendants raised money by selling citizenship for the meager sum of 100 drachmas. The baths, theater, aqueduct, and other ruins are nestled in pine

The main avenue in Phaselis, a major trading post in ancient times, is still busy.

groves around three natural harbors that lend themselves nicely to the lazy contemplation of past civilizations.

Several pleasant seaside villages are nearby. Small, peaceful **Adrasan** skirts a placid bay; several trout restaurants at one end of town serve meals at rustic tables set alongside — and even in — a rushing stream. The somewhat ramshackle village of **Olympos** is behind the beach just outside the ruins, and residents have earned notoriety by providing accommodation in treehouses. **Çıralı,** a hamlet just east along the beach, offers standard amenities.

Antalya

Busy Antalya, 50 km (30 miles) east of Phaselis, was one of the major cities of ancient Pamphylia, settled more than a thousand years before the Christian era by Greek refugees

Historical contrasts: in Antalya a modern statue of "Father Turk" is backed by ancient Yivli Minare.

fleeing from the sack of Troy. Antalya and its now-ruined, neighboring Pamphylian cities of Perge, Aspendos, and Side then passed through the hands of the Persians and Alexander the Great before becoming a sleepy backwater of the Roman Empire.

What will strike you first about Antalya is not its ancient past but its heady involvement with the here and now. Turkey's fastest-growing city is spreading in pell mell fashion over a plateau beneath the Toros mountain range. However, it's **Kaleici,** the old town surrounding the harbor, that will be of most interest to visitors.

Antalya's most famous landmarks crown the bluffs that surround the harbor. The stone **Saat Kulesi** (clocktower) is built into a fragment of the Roman and Ottoman walls, near the so-called Castle Gate and the entrance to the bazaar. **Mehmet Paşa Cami,** a mosque in front of the clocktower, was built in the 16th century, while a much earlier mosque nearby is most famous for its distinctive **Yivli Minare** (Fluted Minaret); the mosque itself is now a municipal art gallery and the courtyards of its adjoining medrese (theological school) have been glassed over to accommodate shops. To the south, along Atatürk Caddesi, is **Hadrian's**

Gate, a rather pompous, three-arched monument built to honor the emperor's visit to the city in A.D. 130. **Hıdırlık Kulesi,** a stone tower from the same era that may have once served as a lighthouse, is set at one end of a garden that affords occasional glimpses of the sea.

Narrow cobblestone lanes wind down toward the harbor from the top of the bluff. Many of the Ottoman houses, built in the 19th century and recently restored (at times a bit too quaintly), now accommodate shops and pansiyons. Above the rooftops rises the **Kesık Minare** (Broken Minaret), an eclectic structure that has served as a Roman temple, a Byzantine church, and an Ottoman mosque. The downhill walk ends on the quays of the harbor, where Antalyans like to come for an evening promenade.

The Antalya Museum

The Antalya Müzesi is at the western edge of the town center and houses an outstanding collection of archaeological artifacts. Many of the holdings are from the ruins at nearby Perge (see page 105) and range from a game board to statuary to a pantheon, reassembled here in its entirety. Other curiosities of local

Three grand arches frame Hadrian's Gate in Antalya, built in honor of a visit from the emperor of the Roman Empire.

origin include Lycian coins from the seventh century B.C., some of the first coinage to ever be minted, and bones said to be those of Saint Nicholas (see pages 98–99). More skeletal remains (of a prehistoric man), recline poetically in a broken funeral urn.

Ruins of the Antalyan Coast

An excursion into the mountains and along the coastline near Antalya brings you to four ancient cities, some remarkable for their settings, some for the extent of their remains, and some for both.

Termessos

Atop a mountain 37 km (23 miles) northwest of Antalya and in the midst of a national park, Termessos is certainly one of the most dramatically situated ruins anywhere. The city's impregnable position atop a crag stopped even Alexander the Great, who determined that a foray up to the city in a shower of boulders the citizenry launched from the ramparts above was unwise. The climb up to the city is still arduous,

> **Be prepared to remove your shoes when entering a private home; not to do so is a rude offense.**

and brings you to well-preserved ruins that are all the more evocative because of the mountainsides looming all around them. The setting of the **theater,** one of its sides at the edge of a deep gorge and another built into a cliff, is as dramatic as any performance that might have been acted out on its stage. The theater steals the show at Termessos, but many other structures are remarkable as well: A large gymnasium adjoins extensive baths with an elaborate water-collection system, and beyond an odeion and temple complex a hillside is eerily littered with more than a hundred tombs.

*Monumental structures attest to the glory of ancient Perge,
but evidence of everyday life is just as evocative.*

Perge

This city that is so well represented in the Antalya Museum
is 22 km (14 miles) east of Antalya, on Route 400. The coast
here is backed by a broad plane, and Perge, accordingly, is
not as spectacularly situated as Termessos. Even so, Perge is
unusually well-preserved, and its copious ruins include an
agora in which the shops still retain their mosaic flooring and
streets that are rutted by chariot wheels. These remains of the
ordinary make it is easy to get a sense of everyday life in the
once bustling town. Monumental Perge is still standing, too,
and its stadium and theater are both massive.

Aspendos

Aspendos is another 31 km (19 miles) east of Perge. Between
these two ancient cities is a modern-day settlement, **Belek,** a

purpose-built golf and beach resort backed by dense woods that have become a haven for ornithologists as well. Pride of place in Aspendos goes to its **theater,** built to Roman designs in the second century B.C. and claimed by many to be the best-preserved theater in the ancient world. The stage, stage house, seats, and portico under which spectators gathered in the event of rain are still here, looking much as they did thousands of years ago. The theater was still in such good repair centuries after its construction that the Selçuks used it for housing when they occupied the city in the 13th century; notice the distinctive Selçuk zigzag plasterwork over the stage. The theater continues to host performances during the annual summer Aspendos Opera and Ballet Festival. High above the theater, on the acropolis, stands a nymphaeum and a basilica; in the distance you can see what remains of an aqueduct that once carried water to the city from mountain springs.

Side

Side, another 22 km (14 miles) east of Aspendos, is two cities: a resort given to the worst excesses of gimcrack tourism, and a ruined port city evocatively set on a stony headland beside the sea. Walking through the monumental gates or looking up

The amphitheater at Aspendos is believed by many to be the best-preserved theater in the ancient world.

From the sands at Side, enjoy the same sunsets as the lovelorn Anthony and Cleopatra.

the theater's tiers of 20,000 seats, it is quite possible to envision Side (which means pomegranate) as the trysting place of Anthony and Cleopatra. It was also the center of a thriving slave trade. Of the ill-fated lovers it must be said that it was not the romance of Side's seaside setting that brought them here; rather, the Egyptian queen was trying to strike a deal with Anthony for the timber that

> **When enjoying a traditional bath and rubdown in a hamam, it is customary to remain wrapped in a towel, a *pestemal*.**

still carpets the mountainsides to the north of the city. The Temples of Athena and Apollo are especially picturesque, poised as they are at the end of the peninsula above the town's much-patronized beaches.

Alanya

Most of this seaside city, 75 km (47 miles) east of Antalya, is relatively new. Though a settlement was already well-established here in 44 B.C., when Anthony presented Alanya to Cleopatra, the heyday came much later, when the Selçuk sultan Alaeddin Keykubad established his summer residence here in 1221.

The older city crowns a peninsula where Ottoman houses cluster beneath the 6 km (4 miles) of walls and 150 towers that surround the kale (castle). The most substantial structures within the enclosure are those of the inner fortress, which shelters a ruined Byzantine church decorated with sixth-century frescoes. More popular, though, are the ramparts that afford a magnificent view and are said to have once been used by executioners to push prisoners to their deaths on the rocks below.

Far below, the harborside **Kızılkule** (Red Tower) is slotted with openings through which archers once shot arrows at invading ships. Around it stretches miles of beaches and the modern city, which in its more boisterous tourist precincts encourages the sort of debauchery that in days gone by would have been punishable by a leap from the castle heights. Another modern diversion is the **Alanya Müzesi** (Alanya Museum), built around a shady garden and housing some artifacts from nearby ruins, including a tablet inscribed in Phoenician, as well as kilims and Ottoman furnishings. The nearby **Damlataş** (Cave of Dripping Stones) affords a glance at some weird stalagmites, and its moist warmth is said to be beneficial to asthma sufferers.

CAPPADOCIA AND KONYA

A strange landscape shaped over millions of years and a busy, no-nonsense Turkish city may seem to have little in common, but Cappadocia and Konya are both imbued with a strong sense of spirituality. One offers its primitive cave churches and the other its monument to the mystical whirling dervishes. Both provide experiences that may well transform you.

Cappadocia

Nature and no small amount of human zeal has shaped Cappadocia, the most magical place you are ever likely to encounter. Over millions of years, volcanic eruptions have covered this region, deep in the mountainous center of Central Anatolia, in deep layers of ash and mud that has solidified into tufta. This soft rock, shaped by the elements into whimsically conical spires called fairy chimneys, proved to be

> In Turkey, it is considered impolite to point the soles of your shoes at someone.

heaven-sent when the early inhabitants embraced Christianity — and found that their faith put them at odds with Romans, Arabs, and even other Christians. Digging into the pliant tufta, they were able to build secret churches, dwellings, and entire underground cities that could harbor as many as 20,000 souls in safety from marauding raiders.

Even in times of peace, cave dwellings tucked into verdant valleys proved to lend themselves ideally to a monastic lifestyle, such as that espoused by Saint Basil, who was born in Cappadocia. Over the years, the ease of digging into the soft tufta has made troglodytes of most Cappadocians, whatever their religious convictions. Every village in the region is, at least in part, a community of caves etched out of weirdly shaped outcroppings. What awaits visitors, especially in the triangle between Ürgüp, Göreme, and Avanos, is a landscape that is nothing short of bizarre, and all the more fascinating for it.

Cappodocia lends itself especially well to exploration on foot, and aside from its distinctive caves and geological formations, the orchards, fields, and forested river valleys invite unhurried walks. In your wanderings you will have the pleasure of encountering Cappodocians, who are often on horseback or behind a plow pulled by a mule. They may well offer you some local wine and tell you where to a find a hidden cave church.

Ürgüp and Nearby Villages

Nevşehir is the largest town in Cappadocia, though Ürgüp, 23 km (14 miles) east, is far more appealing and much better equipped to accommodate travelers who come to marvel at the local scenery. Tucked into a canyon beneath cliffs riddled with cave dwellings, Ürgüp is especially well-situated to bring you face to face with the rather extraordinary realities of Cappadocian life. Ürgüp would be appealing even without its cave dwellings, though, given its cobbled streets lined with handsome houses built by the town's Greek settlers, and its lively little commercial center.

Ürgüp is within reach of several likewise remarkable villages. **Mustafapaşa** is not only near the Gomede Valley and its cave churches, but the village itself is an appealing mix of Greek and Selçuk architecture. Most of the old Greek houses here have been empty since the Greek-Turkish population exchanges of 1923. **Ortahisar** huddles beneath a fantastic, 85-m- (240-ft-) high rock formation riddled with cave dwellings. At one time this cave-riddled rock comprised the entire village, and for a small fee you can explore the former dwellings and lookouts, long since abandoned for the more

The rocky villages of Cappadocia, such as Üçhisar, have a look of fantasy to them.

The early Christians found the cliffs of Göreme to be the ideal setting for monasticism.

conventional buildings below for reasons of safety. **Üçhisar** has outgrown the cave-etched rock, topped with a fortress, that rises from the center of the current village; a climb to its airy heights rewards you with views over much of Cappadocia.

Göreme

This small town, 7 km (4 miles) northwest of Ürgüp, has one big attraction: the **Göreme Açik Hava Müzesi** (Göreme Open Air Museum). The former monastic community, dug into cliffs above a verdant valley, was endowed with more than 30 churches from the ninth through 12th centuries, and many of them are decorated with primitive, though strikingly beautiful, frescoes.

The best-preserved cave church in Cappadocia is here, the **Karanlık Kilise** (Dark Church), and its frescoes have been brilliantly restored. All of the churches are beautiful in their simplicity. Most take their names from an object or image contained in their cramped one-room interiors. Çarıklı Kilise (Sandal Church) is named for the footprints imbedded in the floor, said to be those of Christ. Yılanlı Kilise (Dragon Church) contains a fresco of St. George slaying the dragon. (Another fresco in this church depicts a full-breasted but hirsute Saint Onuphurius, who was allegedly so beautiful that men could not leave her alone. According to the story, when she asked for divine intervention, she was given a beard and moustache.)

Zelve, 6 km (4 miles) northeast, is much less crowded than Göreme, and exploration of its cliffside churches and dwellings requires more of a sense of adventure — as well as a flashlight and the ability to burrow and climb.

The Underground Cities

Kaymaklı and **Derinkuyu,** respectively 71 and 80 km (43 and 49 miles) southwest of Ürgup, are the strangest habitations in Cappadocia. These vast underground complexes descend hundreds of feet into the earth and were elaborately equipped with dormitories, sanitation systems, kitchens, wine-pressing facilities, cemeteries, and other amenities. As a result, they could house thousands of refugees for years on end. Comforting as the cities must have been for those in need of a safe haven, be warned that the narrow passages can quickly induce claustrophobia. Another underground city, **Ozkonak,** has only relatively recently been discovered near **Avanos;** excavations are still underway and visitors can enter only a few passages. Avanos, an appealing town on the wine-colored Kizilirmak river, Turkey's longest, has long manufactured distinctive onyx pottery and jewelry.

The Ihlara Valley

For centuries, this gorge, about 100 km (60 miles) southwest of Ürgüp, was a lost world. More than 100 m (330 ft) deep and well off the beaten path, the valley provided a perfect hideout for early Christians. Over the years, inhabitants dug more than 100 churches and monasteries into the cliff walls. Still less discovered than other places in Cappadocia, and reached by a steep wooden staircase from the village of Ihlara, the valley now provides excellent hikes along its 14-km (9-mile) length and the opportunity to climb into the 15 churches that are open to the public.

Konya

Konya, on the vast Anatolian plains 142 km (88 miles) north of Ihlara, was a Hittite settlement, an important Roman outpost, a center of the early Christian church, and a Selçuk capital. Despite this long history, Konya would have long ago settled into relative obscurity were it not for the Sufi mystic Celaleddin Rumi, who became known as the Mevlâna and founded the sect known as Mevlei, or Whirling Dervishes.

The Mevlâna's tomb and the adjoining Mevlâna Museum are among the most important pilgrimage destinations in Turkey and the Islamic world, visited by thousands who come to pay homage to the great mystic and teacher. Rumi was born in Central Asia in 1207 and fled to Konya when he was 20. Here he met his mentor, a wandering dervish named Sems-ı-Tabriz. Rumi devoted

A foot bridge carries travelers over the river that cuts through the lush floor of the Ilhara Valley.

Clusters of trees rise above the rich plains of Central Anatolia, a far cry from İstanbul.

himself to study with Sems and was inconsolable when his master disappeared (possibly murdered by jealous colleagues of Rumi). Turning himself to Sufi teachings, he was inspired to write several volumes of spiritual poetry, the Mathnawi. He became an ardent teacher, encouraging his growing band of disciples to embrace love and charity, as well as such enlightened concepts as respect for women.

The brotherhood that Rumi founded is best known to outsiders for its distinctive and beautiful *sema,* a ceremony in which dancers whirl to symbolically free themselves of earthly ties. The position of the arms, with the right arm extending to heaven and the left to the floor, reassuringly conveys the notion that the dancers are conduits through which the grace of God is flowing to humanity. The dancers' garments also have symbolic significance: The hat represents a tombstone,

the cloak is the tomb (and is shed during the dance to represent escape from earthly bonds), and the white skirt is the funeral shroud.

Though the Mevlei have been forbidden to practice openly since all religious brotherhoods were banned during the Republic's early years, the government has continued to promote the sema for its folkloric merit; today, an increasing number of the dancers also openly follow the teachings of the Mevlâna. The dervishes perform in Konya during an annual December festival, though you can see them at other times in İstanbul and elsewhere throughout Turkey (see page 42).

View the ritual of the Whirling Dervishes at the Mevlâna mosque in Konya.

The Mevlâna Müzesi

Beneath a distinctive blue dome spreads the original 13th-century monastery of the dervishes and the mausoleum of the Mevlâna. The entranceway is rather humbling, reached as it is past the dervishes' tiny monastic cells and the gardens that once sustained the community. Inside, a more monumental atmosphere prevails: Beyond the reading room, where the dervishes would once congregate to study the Koran, is the **mausoleum;** the tomb of the Melvâna rests on a pedestal, surrounded by the coffins of his eldest son and his father. The adjoining circular hall is the *semahane,* where the sema was originally performed. Reed flutes and other instruments that accompany the dance are on display, as are some exquisite and extraordinarily rare Selçuk carpets presented to the Melvâna as gifts.

Elsewhere in Konya

Of the several mosques and seminaries that surround the Mevlâna complex, the most enchanting is the **Büyük Karatay Medrese,** a Selçuk theological school that is extensively and enchantingly tiled. The dome is decorated with a dramatic representation of the firmaments and was used at one time for astronomical study. A collection of rare tiles and other ceramics are on display in adjoining galleries, grouped around a fountain-cooled courtyard.

This medrese and the nearby **İnce Minare Medrese** (Seminary of the Slender Minaret) are graced with unusually elegant Selçuk portals, both of which are ornately tiled in geometric patterns and — a reminder that these were among the first structures the nomadic Selçuks undertook to design and build — resemble the entrances to tents. The eponymous minaret of the Ince Minare Medrese is beautifully tiled but was severely truncated by a bolt of lightning a hundred years ago; inside is a collection of stone and wood work, much of it salvaged from a nearby Selçuk palace.

Konya's second most imposing edifice is the **Alaaddin Cami,** a 13th-century Selçuk mosque that commands a hill north of the Mevlâna Müzesi. Reflecting its Syrian design, the massive interior is forested with 42 columns, topped with Roman capitals. What you may well remember most about this mosque, however, is the view it affords, past its surrounding park back to the dome that shelters the earthly remains of the Mevlâna.

WHAT TO DO

Exploring the remains of classical civilizations and enjoying the splendors of the Ottoman Empire, with some time off to relax on a beach, could keep you happily occupied in Turkey. Sooner or later, you'll also find yourself immersed in a wealth of other activities (see Guides and Tours on page 158 for some opportunities to combine travel with learning and pursuing special interests).

SHOPPING

Most towns of any size in Turkey have a *bedestan,* or covered bazaar, at their center, and this warren of stalls is often the major shopping precinct. Any number of small shops usually spill out onto the sidewalks of the streets surrounding the

bazaar. A street market also usually springs up somewhere near the center of town once or twice a week, selling fresh fish, meat, and produce alongside ordinary household items.

The most essential tool a visitor can bring to these venues is at least a modicum of skill at bargaining. This age-old art is both an intrinsic

For those who enjoy hunting for eclectic souvenirs, Turkey's traditional brass and copper wares can be true finds.

part of shopping and a social custom; in fact, it's fair to say that not to engage in at least some negotiating is rude; doing so effectively, however, can take both practice and mettle. See the box below for some tips.

Bazaars

In these mainstays of Turkish commerce, a walk down crowded lanes past stalls selling everything from spices to mops is tinged

---

The Art of Bargaining

While there are no hard-and-fast rules governing how to strike a deal with a wily merchant, remember two basics: However clever you think you are, the seller has the advantage of years of experience and will inevitably gain the upper hand (i.e., it's safe to say a profit will be made no matter how hard you bargain); and, the one sure way to infuriate any seller is to engage in hard bargaining when you have no intention of buying — don't begin the process unless you are actually interested in leaving the premises with the item in question under your arm!

Begin by asking the merchant how much the item costs. Whatever the response, your next step is to say "too much," best accompanied by a look of disappointment. The seller will probably come back with a lower price, perhaps sighing that this figure is being extended only because it is the first or last sale of the day or because it's clear that you really want the item in question. Hold firm and say the price is still too high. A new offer will be forthcoming, at which point it is time to make your final counteroffer. Whatever the price with which you come back, the seller is all but obligated to add a bit to it. If you arrive at a final price that is half or 60% of what the seller originally proposed, you've done a good job and it's time to close the deal over a glass of çay (tea).

119

with no small amount of exotic flavor. Bazaars supply Turkish households with essentials, and those in towns on well-worn travel circuits also cater to visitors with all manner of souvenirs.

Your wanderings through the following centers of commerce are likely to be especially rewarding, either for the experience or the quality of the goods with which you emerge, or both.

In İstanbul

The **Egyptian Bazaar,** also known as the Spice Market, houses an especially appealing selection of nuts, spices, dried fruits, and the candy known as Turkish Delight beneath its atmospheric, 17th-century vaulted ceilings (see page 34). The **Grand Bazaar** is perhaps best approached for its colorful atmosphere rather than as a bargain-filled paradise, since tourist-oriented goods tend to be a bit tawdry (of the cheap fezzes and lamps shaped like the Blue Mosque variety) and many of the more solid goods offered are ordinary items (including an inordinate number of T-shirts emblazoned with American lingo) geared to locals. Some exceptions include the gold jewelry and antiques sold in shops near the center of the bazaar, which has always been the precinct of better shops and high prices; some silver goods, especially those made and sold in the northeastern corner in what is known as the Kalicilar Han; and the old books and prints in the Old Book Bazaar, just beyond the western gate (see page 36). The **Flower Arcade** and **Fish Market,** just off Galatasaray Meydanı in Pera, are unusually colorful precincts; in the Fish Market you will also find pastry shops and fast-food stalls (see page 43).

Elsewhere

The bedestan in **Bursa** is one of Turkey's most atmospheric bazaars, dating to the 13th century but now housed in a

The Grand Bazaar offers more than a wide array of goods — its most notable feature is the colorful atmosphere.

beautifully restored 19th-century structure; thick cotton towels, a local specialty, are an especially good buy here (see page 125). In **Edirne,** the bedestan and adjoining Ali Paşa Bazaar are authentic marketplaces where you will find yourself rubbing shoulders with what seems to be most of the town's population, especially on Saturdays (see page 53). On the resort circuit, **Marmaris** is equipped with a large and well-stocked bazaar, catering as it does to the many visitors who sail over from Rhodes for the day.

What to Buy

Carpets and Kilims. You probably won't leave Turkey without at least one, so look forward to your purchase of a floor covering as an enjoyable experience. Walk into any carpet shop and abandon yourself to the dealer. You will be offered a seat and a cup of tea, and what can only be described as a

No visit to Turkey is complete without at least a few hours of friendly haggling over an intricately patterned rug.

show will begin. Rug after rug will be laid at your feet; a savvy dealer will soon detect the size, materials, colors, and patterns that seem to be most appealing to you, and eventually bring out only items that match those criteria, narrowing the choices until it seems you must select at least one. Many connoisseurs say the best rugs have long since been brought to İstanbul (which is probably true of the most expensive pieces); others insist you can still find treasures in smaller towns and villages. Since most carpets are made in Central Anatolia, shops near the sources in Cappadocia tend to have an excellent selection, especially of inexpensive new, woolen kilims made by local villagers. In İstanbul, you can ease into carpet-buying in some of the lower key shops of Sultanahmet; those in the İstanbul Handicrafts Centre, next to the Yeşil Ev Hotel (see page 174), are unusually genteel and the goods are of excellent quality.

Copper. Candlesticks, teapots, trays, and samovars handsomely handcrafted from copper were once the mainstay of a bride's dowry, and these items have found their way to many an antiques shop (the Mediterranean resorts of Kaş and Kalkan (see pages 95 and 96) are especially well-stocked with authentic copper pieces). Likewise, copper items of modern manufacture — machine-made with a thin sheath of copper over a less expensive alloy — are among the more appealing displays of many bazaars.

Some rules of thumb: If it's authentically old, it will be expensive; if it's new, it will be quite inexpensive, but

> **A term bound to launch you into bargaining mode:** *Fiyati ne kadar?* **(How much does it cost?)**

attractive despite its lack of provenance; and whether old or new, make sure any copper cooking vessel is lined with tin (a good merchant can send you to a reliable tinsmith who can do so inexpensively).

Ceramics. It's been centuries since the factories of İznik stopped manufacturing the town's famous tiles on a large scale, although a few artisans continue the craft; the tourist board (see page 170) can lead you to shops selling the very limited supply and also to whatever studios are welcoming visitors at the time of your visit. The town of Kütahya southeast of İznik is currently Turkey's largest producer of ceramic tiles, and you can find them, of good quality and in attractive patterns, in shops throughout the country.

The same earth that thrust up the fantastic formations of Cappadocia also yields a bounty of onyx that shows up in bowls, boxes, and every other conceivable creation; the old town of Avanos (see page 113) is chock-full of shops selling onyx and pottery made from red clay from the banks of the aptly named Red River, which rushes through town.

Clothing. You'll have no trouble finding imitations of top Western designers in markets all over Turkey. For a look at fashionable Turkish couture, step into the shops along and around Istiklal Caddesi in İstanbul (nearby Rumeli Caddesi and Halâskârgazi Caddesi are especially fashionable shopping streets); the Galleria in the suburb of Ataköy on the Asian side is one of several suburban-style malls that outfit the well-to-do with local and foreign fashions.

Carpet Caveats

Step into any carpet shop — and sidewalk touts will extend innumerable invitations to do so — and you will soon be schooled in weaves, knots, dyes, motifs, and many other details that will render a well-informed novice. A few things to keep in mind before you take the plunge:

A kilim, the omnipresent Turkish floor covering, is pile-less and flat-woven, and its pattern is clearly visible on the reverse side. Be wary of claims that dyes are natural. Synthetic dyes have been used for well over a century, and a rug made with natural dyes is likely to be quite rare and expensive. If a dealer insists that a rug is an antique (which again is unlikely), ask for proof — on the other hand, claims that a rug has been made from old saddlebags or pieces of old kilims may well be true and the resulting article, in fact, can be uniquely beautiful.

To ensure colors will not run, rub a wet white cloth over the fabric — if it picks up color, you know that inexpensive, non-durable dyes have been used. If the material is pure wool, a strand will crumble when lighted; pure silk will turn immediately to fine ash. Smell a rug to see if you can detect the scent of vinegar — sometimes it is applied to fade colors and "age" a new rug to add antique value. A reputable dealer will encourage you to perform these tests.

If a rug is hand-woven, the pattern and knots that show on the reverse side will be slightly irregular and the fringe is likely to be uneven as well.

Patterns and colors are rich in symbolic meaning, so ask the salesman to explain what they mean.

A reputable shop will provide a detailed receipt and be willing to ship the rug for you. Have it sent UPS, FedEx, or via some other international service and ask for a shipping receipt so that you can track the shipment with the courier once you get back home.

Bursa is famous for silk and cotton manufacture, and a number of shops clustered around its atmospheric bazaar sell scarves, vests, and other clothing made from these materials.

Leather Goods. Turkey produces fine leather, though most of the leather goods you see may well be in the form of chain purses, lipstick cases, key holders, wallets and other inexpensive items stacked high in every bazaar. You will encounter tailors offering "made-to-measure" leather wear in many resorts. Side (see page 106), on the Mediterranean Coast, seems to have sold its soul to such enterprises, and almost every other shop in the once-quaint old town now promises to hand stitch the leather item of your choice within a few hours; though the workmanship and quality of the leather is often questionable, if you stick to a simple design you will probably walk away with a durable, unique and affordable garment.

Spices. A popular item in every bazaar, these often come in handy assortment packets. Beware, however, of seemingly good deals on saffron — the least expensive comes from Turkey, but saffron from Iran is of far superior quality.

And Keep an Eye Out for... Glass "eyes" often worn as pendants to ward off the evil eye; curly-tipped slippers; felt fezzes; hookah water pipes (the best have glass bowls and wood or brass hardware); meerschaum pipes carved from porous stone; attractive vests, slippers, and fez-style caps fashioned from old kilims; thick cotton bath towels made in Bursa — all of these are easily portable and evocative mementos and are readily available in many bazaars and tourist shops throughout the country (in İstanbul, the streets around Sultanhamet Square house many higher quality shops of this nature).

OUTDOOR ACTIVITIES

With long summers that stretch from late April well into late October, Turkey provides a number of outdoor pursuits.

Excursion boats along the rivers and lakes are a great way to see the sights and enjoy a cooling aquatic breeze.

Ballooning

The most dramatic way to enjoy the spectacular vistas of Cappadocia is to make an ascent in a hot-air balloon. This memorable and expensive experience is provided by Kapadokya Balloons in Göreme, Tel. 384-271-2442.

Birdwatching

As a stop on migratory routes between Europe, Asia, and Africa, Turkey is rich terrain for birds and birders. Some places to see winged creatures include Kuşcenneti National Park (the name translates as "Bird Paradise") near Bursa; the woodlands behind the Mediterranean resort of Belek (see page 105); and the shores of Lake Köyceğiz, near Dalyan (see page 87). For more information, contact: Doğal Hayatı Koruma Derneği (National Wildlife Protection Association), P.K. 18 Bebek-İstanbul, Tel. 212-279-0139; fax 212-279-5544.

Golf

While links are relatively scarce in Turkey, you will find a few around major cities and resorts. In fact, the new, purpose-built resort of Belek, just east of Antalya, has four 18-hole courses, some of which are part of luxury beach hotel

Getting Soaked

Turks have indulged in the cleansing and relaxation to be had in a hamam, or bath, for centuries. Almost every town of any size has at least one of these establishments, though non-Turks will probably feel most comfortable at those in major cities and towns on well-beaten tourist paths. You'll find that almost all that have hamams will either a separate section for women or specified hours for men and women. Rates should be clearly posted at the reception desk upon entering; if they're not, simply ask.

Upon entering, you will undress in a cubicle and wrap yourself in a large, thin cloth (a pestemal), which, at risk of appearing immodest, you should wear throughout the ritual (you will be handed a dry towel at the end of the bath). You will first enter a sauna-like chamber for a pore-cleansing, pre-wash sweat, and then the large main room, the hararet, which is usually domed and tiled. After cleansing yourself in basins on the sides of the room, you will be laid upon a heated stone (gobek tasi) and soaped and massaged with a kese, a sort of large, exfoliating mitt. Before the final rinse, your masseur will skillfully blow a soapy cloth into a balloon-like ball and give you a refreshing lather. Returning to your cubicle, you will be offered tea or a cool beverage and invited to sit and relax; in some hamams, you will be offered the chance (for an additional fee) to top off the bath with a deep tissue oil massage.

In İstanbul, you can be luxuriously introduced to this local custom at Cağaloğlu Hamami at Kazı Gürkan Caddesi 34, convenient to the sights and hotels of Sultanhamet; it's open from 8am–10pm.

complexes (see page 105). Two courses near İstanbul are Classis Country and Golf Club, Tel. 212-748-4600, and Kemer Country and Golf Club, Tel. 212-239-7913.

Hiking

One of the best hiking trails in Turkey is the Lycian Way, which dips and climbs through the mountains along the Mediterranean Coast from Ölüdeniz to Antalya. Spectacular views, remote beaches, dense pine forests, and ancient ruins are among the attractions you'll come to along the route. A Lycian Way guidebook, in English, is available in newsstands in most Mediterranean resorts. Other trails along the Mediterranean Coast include those that cut deep into the spectacular Saklikent Gorge near the ancient city of Tlos (see page 92), climb Mt. Olympos, and crisscross Termessos National Park, in which you'll come to the dramatic ruins of the ancient city of the same name.

The slopes of Mount Uludağ near Bursa are laced with hiking trails. Hiking is one of the best ways to enjoy the scenery of Cappadocia and trails follow the floors of its many valleys past fantastic rock formations and cliffs etched with centuries-old cave churches and monastic complexes.

Horseback Riding

Cappadocia is especially well-suited to riding, and several local companies rent horses and lead excursions. For more information, contact the tourist offices in Ürgüp and Göreme (see page 170).

Sailing and Yachting

Many travelers say the only way to explore the Aegean and Mediterranean coasts, with their many coves and inlets, is by boat. Some of the major marinas are those in İzmir, Çeşme,

Kuşadası, Bodrum, Marmaris, Fethiye, and Antalya; the tourist offices in each can provide information on facilities and fees (see page 170). Currents and winds along the coasts can be strong; for conditions, tune into shortband waves VHF 16 and 67 for broadcasts in English at 6:30 and 10:30am, and 2:30, 4:30 and 6:30pm.

Many companies offer cruises along the coast in a traditional Turkish craft, a gulet. You can arrange cruises with local operators in most resorts, with the largest number located in Bodrum and Marmaris. Among foreign operators with which you can arrange a trip, usually about a week in advance, are: Overseas Adventure Travel, Tel. 800-221-0814 in

Up, up, and away — taking to the skies with a parasail or a hot-air balloon is becoming a popular tourist activity.

the US; Sunsail, Tel. 01705-222222 in the UK; and Wiltrans, Tel. 02-9255-0899 in Australia.

Scuba Diving

The abundance of underwater antiquities makes it illegal to dive in many of the waters off Turkey. You can, however, dive in several authorized areas, most notably in the waters off Bodrum and the Mediterranean resort of Kaş. Dive shops abound in both, as do several dive schools in and around Bodrum. For more information, contact the Turkish Diving Federation, Ulus Ishane, A. Blok., 303-304, Ulus, Ankara, Tel. 312-310-4136; fax: 312-310-8288.

Swimming

The most enjoyable swimming is from the fine beaches along the Mediterranean Coast; the best of these are at İstuzu, Patara, and Ölüdeniz, of which only Ölüdeniz is likely to become crowded, while at Olympos and Phaselis you can enjoy the memorable experience of swimming from ruin-backed strands. On the Aegean Coast, you will find especially nice beaches and clear waters at Ayvalik, Çeşme, and Didyma; on the ever-popular Bodrum Peninsula, you may well want to escape the crush and seek out the relatively secluded beaches at Bagla and Gümüşlük.

> While nudity is prohibited on Turkish beaches, topless and nude bathing is common on isolated strands.

Pollution will keep you out of the waters in the immediate vicinity of İstanbul, but beaches on the nearby Princes Islands are quite pleasant. The strands on the northern and western shores of Heybeli are especially quiet and nice.

Windsurfing

The broad bays around Çeşme, Bodrum, and Marmaris are especially well-suited to windsurfing. You'll find rental equipment and instruction at each location.

ENTERTAINMENT

On a high note, the State Symphony Orchestra, State Opera, and State Ballet perform in İstanbul, often at Atatürk Kültür Merkezi on Taksim Square, Tel. 212-251-5600. The city enjoys a cultural flowering in late June through mid-July, when the İstanbul International Festival stages dance, opera, and classical music performances throughout the city; the tourist office can provide details (see page 170) or contact: İstanbul Foundation for Culture and Arts, İstiklal Caddesi 146, Beyoğlu 80070; Tel. 212-293-3133. For other music and arts festivals around the country, see page 132.

Can't come to Turkey without hearing some traditional music and seeing some belly-dancing? Take heart, as any number of establishments provide evenings of dance and music for visitors. In İstanbul, one of the more venerable institutions offering tourist-oriented "Turkish Nights" is

Belly-dancing and traditional music are not hard to find in the myriad of nightspots in İstanbul.

Kervanasary, Cumhuriyet Caddesi 30, Tel. 212-247-1630. In Antalya, 7 Mehmet, in Hasan Subasi Culture Park, is a well known venue for traditional music and dance; Tel. 212-241-4855. You will find several similar establishments, often open only in the summer, on your travels up and down the coast and into Cappadocia; the tourist offices can lead you to shows in a particular region. For a look at an authentic slice of Turkish culture, stop by the Divan Edebiyati Müzesi in İstanbul on the last Sunday of the month at 3pm, when Whirling Dervishes perform their famous dances.

Festivals and Seasonal Events

No matter what time of the year you visit Turkey, your travels may well coincide with a festival celebrating some aspect of the country's rich culture. Here are some of the major festivals.

January In Selçuk, camels match mettle in the annual Camel Wrestling Festival.

April The İstanbul International Film Festival and International İzmir Film Festival screen new films from Turkey and elsewhere.

April–May In Emirgan, a suburb of İstanbul, the Tulip Festival celebrates a passion for this flower that dates back to Ottoman times.

May Marmaris opens the summer season with the International Yacht Festival.

June Ürgüp, in Cappadocia, matches the produce of the region's vineyards with wines from around the world at the International Wine Competition; boats sail down the Aegean Coast from İstanbul to İzmir in the International Offshore Races; in Edirne, wrestlers coated in oil compete in the Traditional Kirkpinar Wrestling Tournament; Çeşme breaks out in song during the Çeşme International Song Contest.

June–July The İstanbul Arts Festival hosts classical musicians from around the world; Bursa, İzmir and Marmaris celebrate local folk arts with festivals of dance and music.

August Troy captures its ancient glory with readings from Homer and a beauty contest in which a modern Helen is selected; the İzmir International Fair celebrates local culture.

September The International Grape Harvest Festival in Ürgüp features tastings of local wines; the International Akdeniz Song Contest in Antalya brings together the finest voices in Turkey.

October The film festival in Antalya honors Turkish film makers; the International Bodrum Cup attracts yachtsmen from around the world.

November The International Yacht Race in Marmaris is Turkey's last sailing competition of the season.

December In Demre, the International St. Nicholas Symposium honors the local saint who is known the world over as Santa Claus; the Mevlâna Commemoration Ceremony in Konya features performances of the Whirling Dervishes.

In the resorts along the Aegean and Mediterranean coasts you will have no trouble finding discos and dance clubs that throb late into the summer nights. A slightly more somber, but highly atmospheric, ambiance prevails at the Pera Palace in İstanbul,

> **Two important words to keep in mind at sights and attractions:** *acik* (open) and *kapali* (closed).

Meşrutiyet Caddesi 98, Tel. 212-251-4560 (see page 43), where you can enjoy a cocktail in the Orient Express Bar and relive the days when this 19th-century hostelry hosted royalty and celebrities.

TRAVELING WITH CHILDREN

Turkey has some places bound to engage young travelers, no matter how bored they are with museums and ruins. **In İstanbul,** the kids might enjoy Topkapı Palace, with its armor, intriguing harem, refreshing gardens, and city and sea views; a ferry ride on the Bosporus; and descents into underground cisterns and walks through the exotic bazaars.

On the Aegean and Mediterranean Coasts, visit Ephesus, with its extensive and well-preserved ruins that entice travelers of all ages; the ruins at Ayvalık, Olympos, and Phaselis, where a blast from the past is combined with great beaches; Dalyan, which is only a boat trip away from beautiful Lake Köyceğiz, ancient Kaunos and long, empty İstuzu Beach; and Kekova Sound, where boats glide over submerged cities.

In Cappadocia, there are ample opportunities to scramble up and down ladders and hidden staircases through centuries-old churches and monastic complexes at Göreme and elsewhere; the villages of Ortahisar and Üçhisar are topped by lofty, and climbable, rock citadels; and the underground cities of Derinkuyu and Kaymaklı can be explored on eerily fascinating underground passageways.

EATING OUT

The pleasures of the Turkish table are considerable, and travelers unfamiliar with this cuisine will find that it is fresh, delicious, and varied. Fish caught that day, fresh vegetables and herbs, simply grilled chicken and lamb, and creamy yogurt are the mainstays of menus. In fact, a good meal awaits you wherever your travels take you in Turkey.

While street food and snacks are available throughout the day in most of the cities and resorts you are likely to visit, you're most likely to find a full lunch from noon–3pm and dinner from 7–10pm. Except in the most expensive restaurants in large cities, dress is casual.

Even in İstanbul and other large cities, there are fewer full-scale restaurants than there are in European cities. Better restaurants, accordingly, tend to be crowded, so you may want to reserve a table in advance; your hotel will probably be happy to provide this service and arrange for transportation as well. However, you'll probably have no problem finding a café or restaurant in resorts that cater to large numbers of foreign visitors during the warmer months.

Save room for something sweet, as the local bazaar is sure to offer a variety of Turkish Delight.

Where to Eat

Especially in İstanbul and other large cities, you may be a bit overwhelmed by the number and variety of establishments selling the Turkish version of "fast food," often from stand-up counters. *Kebapcı* serve the ubiquitous stable of Turkish cuisine, the kebab; lamb is continually being roasted on a revolving spit, ready to be sliced and skewered with roast vegetables. *Dönercis* serve roast lamb as well, in this case on bread or rice, while *pideci* offer pide, what can only be described as Turkish pizza, a delicious concoction of flat bread topped with meats, vegetables, and cheese.

> Two useful terms in this country that puts a premium on politeness: *lütfen* (please) and *tesekur ederim* (thank you).

When Turks eat a full meal out, it is usually in a *lokanta,* a simple restaurant that caters to workers at lunch and, often, to neighborhood families in the evening. The dozen or so dishes offered at any one time are usually on display in a glass case and can be dished up at your request; most of these places serve one or two meat or fish dishes, often prepared as stews, with vegetable and rice accompaniments.

A full-blown *restoran,* or restaurant, is often only marginally more fancy, but can also be quite elegant. In resorts, restaurant tables often spill onto terraces. You will also find a number of European-style cafés that serve light meals throughout the day, with menus that include a mix of sandwiches, omelets, pide, and kebabs.

What to Eat

A Turkish **breakfast,** often served in even the most modest hotels, is simple and satisfying. It will often include sliced cucumber, olives, tomato, a hard boiled egg, yogurt, a piece of fruit, and a slice or two of bread to be topped with jam or

A group of women in traditional dress bake the type of flat bread that is likely to accompany your meal.

honey. You can usually request fruit juice, and will be offered coffee (Turkish or instant "American" coffee, generally referred to as Nescafé) or tea. If you feel like venturing out, you'll inevitably come upon a counter or cart from which borek, a fluffy cheese pastry, is served.

For **lunch,** you can either seek out lighter fare or a full meal that will be much the same as dinner. **Dinner** inevitably begins with meze, a wide assortment of delicious hot or cold appetizers (see pages 139–140 for some of the meze and other dishes you are likely to find on a typical menu). Meze, in fact, are so satisfying that you may not feel the need to venture any farther onto the menu.

Choices for a main course inevitably include a variety of lamb or chicken dishes; pork is not served in this Muslim country, and when beef makes an appearance it is usually ground. Just about any restaurant, no matter how simple or elaborate, will serve several variations of lamb or chicken kebabs, as well as such staples as manti, a meat-filled ravioli, and kofte, meatballs. Fresh fish, often sea bass and swordfish, is the mainstay of menus along the Aegean and Mediterranean coasts, where restaurants usually display the catch on ice and serve it simply grilled with oil and lemon. Trout is also common, and in the countryside you're likely to encounter the occasional restaurant that raises trout in a pond or stream and serves it at outdoor, tree-shaded tables (in fact, this experience is a good reason to stop at the little Mediterranean resort of Adrasan; see page 101).

Typical vegetable accompaniments are simply steamed broad beans or zucchini, and salad — greens are relatively rare, and a salad often consists of tomatoes, onions, peppers, cucumbers, olives, and perhaps some feta cheese. The most popular desserts are baklava, phyllo pastry drenched in honey, and helva, sesame paste.

Beverages

In this Muslim country many establishments do not serve alcohol. It's easier to come upon establishments serving some alcoholic beverages, often just beer and wine, in resorts than it is in some of the larger cities that are less visited by non-Turks. Turkish wines, many of them grown in Cappadocia and along the

A vendor slices meat for a döner kebab, Turkey's best-known fast food.

Aegean Coast, are becoming more available, and many restaurants serve nothing but local varieties; Cankaya whites from Kavaklidere vineyards are well worth requesting. If you ask for a domestic beer you'll likely be served an Efes Pilsen. Budweiser, Corona, and Heineken are the most widespread imported brands. Similarly, you can buy domestically produced hard spirits such as gin and vodka, and you can find imported spirits in most resorts and in more upscale bars in the larger cities. The alcoholic beverage of local choice, however, is raki, similar to Greek ouzo and, often mixed with water and ice, enjoyed before, during, and after a meal.

> **At public fountains, look for a sign that says *Icilebilir su* (drinking water).**

If you ask for coffee, you may well be served the bland, instant brew that is almost always referred to as Nescafé, despite the brand; if you want something more satisfying, request Turkish coffee, which is usually served *orta şekerli* (medium sweet) or *çok şekerli* (very sweet). Tea, *çay,* is far more common, and you'll probably be charmed by the fact that even shopkeepers dispense it freely to their customers; it is served in small glasses, to which you can add

The day's catch from the Mediterranean will probably be grilled simply and served nice and fresh.

water and sugar, but never milk, as desired. Bottled water is easy to find and is a necessary alternative to tap water.

To Help You Order...

Do you speak English?	**Inglizce biliyormusunz?**
Waiter!	**Lütfen bakar mısmız!**
What would you recommend?	**Ne tavsiye edersiniz?**

To Help You Read the Menu...

Meze (Starters)

Amerikan salatası	a salad of mayonnaise and vegetables
Beyaz penir	goat cheese
Borek	pastry filled with cheese and herbs
Dolması	stuffed grape leaves
Cacık	yogurt with cucumber and garlic
Haydarı	garlic dip
Imam bayıldı	eggplants stuffed with tomato and onion
Mucver	zucchini pancake
Tarama	yogurt with caviar and garlic

Et (Meat)

Döner kebab	sliced roasted lamb
Iskembe	tripe
Iskender Kebab Döner	kebab drenched in yogurt
Karısık ızgara	mixed grill
Piliç	roast chicken
Pitzola	lamb chops
Şiş kofte	grilled lamb meatballs

Balık (Fish)

Ahtapod	octopus	**Kalkan**	turbot
Alabalık	trout	**Karide**	prawns
Barbunya	red mullet	**Kiliç**	swordfish
Hamsi	anchovies	**Midye**	mussels
Kalamar	squid	**Sardalya**	sardines

Sebze (Vegetables)

Bakla	broad beans	**Lahana**	cabbage
Bamya	okra	**Nohut**	chickpeas
Domates	tomatoes	**Patates**	potatoes
Ispanak	spinach	**Patlıcan**	eggplant
Kabak	zucchini	**Salatalık**	cucumber

Tatlı (Dessert)

Dondurma	ice cream
Kadayıf	shredded wheat in syrup
Kadın göbeği	doughnut in syrup
Keşkül	vanilla almond custard
Lokum	Turkish Delight
Pasta	pastry or cake
Sütlac	rice pudding
Tahin	Helvasi Helva

Beverages

Bira	beer
Çay	tea
Kahve	coffee
Maden Suyu	sparkling mineral water
Meyva Suyu	fruit juice
Sarap	wine

HANDY TRAVEL TIPS

An A–Z Summary of Practical Information

ACCOMMODATIONS

In the past couple of decades, a great number of comfortable new hotels have opened throughout Turkey, especially in İstanbul, along the Aegean and Mediterranean coasts, and in Cappadocia. Many international chains have opened hotels, and other new inns occupy restored Ottoman houses and other historic properties. In general, lodgings fall into three categories: hotels *(oteli),* which you'll find in larger towns and cities; motels, common along the Aegean and Mediterranean coasts and, unlike the drive-in hostelries the name connotes to North American travelers, usually more of a resort complex with spacious grounds, often a beach and sports facilities, and simple lodgings that are frequently housed in bungalows; and guest houses *(pansiyons)* which, especially in rural areas, can mean simple, rock-bottom accommodations or, increasingly in the historic quarters of cities and towns, character-filled and comfortable bed-and-breakfast-type lodgings that provide modern amenities in centuries-old surroundings.

Many of these establishments are rated on a somewhat confusing government scale, with HL denoting a luxury establishment and others rated from H1 (a first-class hotel) to H5 (a fifth-class hotel). Technically, the rating reflects the number of amenities offered (in-room bathrooms, elevators, air-conditioning, etc.). However, the star system is strictly objective and does not reflect charm or ambiance, and a highly desirable establishment can be given a lower rating simply because it doesn't offer as many amenities, such as in-room television, as a mediocre establishment next door. In some cities and larger towns, hotels are rated according to a similar system established by the municipality rather than the Turkish government, and standards can vary considerably from place to place. What you can be assured of is that any hotel that is rated will be inspected regularly, and as a result will maintain the rated level of cleanliness and comfort.

To find a hotel that suits your tastes and budget, see Recommended Hotels on page 172, which includes a range of better lodgings, and contact tourist information offices (see page 170), which can provide a list of accommodations in most towns, with addresses, phone and fax numbers, number of rooms, and amenities offered. Once you are in Turkey and have found a lodging that is to your liking, don't be afraid to ask the innkeeper for a recommendation in your next stop — chances are that he or she will know from first-hand experience or hearsay of similarly pleasant establishments elsewhere.

For stays of a week or more in one place, you may want to consider a rental property. These are primarily available in the coastal resorts. Local tourist offices can sometimes provide information on such rentals, and they are sometimes available from overseas tour operators, especially those in the UK; two such outfits with a large number of houses and bungalows along the coast are: Simply Turkey, Kings House, Wood St., Kingston-upon-Thames, Surrey KT1 1UG, Tel. 020-8541-2204; and Sunquest, 23 Prince's St., London W1R 7RG, Tel. 020-7499-9991. Ask for photos (many firms will send a video tape), a contract with terms thoroughly spelled out, and the names of former renters with whom you can speak.

Wherever you stay, prices will be considerably less than they are for similar accommodations in Western Europe and North America. Increasingly, breakfast is included with the price of the room. In most establishments, expect to find single beds; if you want a double bed, request a *Fransiz yatak,* French bed, though these are often not available. While hotels at the higher end of the price scale provide the wall-to-wall carpeting and modern-bath ambiance of modern hotels everywhere, many Turkish hotels are simpler, with tile floors, white-washed walls, and basic plumbing, with a stall shower and Western-style toilet, as opposed to a traditional squat toilet.

I have a reservation. **Reservasyonim var**.

Turkey

I'd like a single/double room.	**Tek/çift yataklı bir oda istiyorum.**
With shower	**Duşlu**
What is the price per night?	**Bir gecelik oda ücreti ne kadar?**
Can I see the room?	**Bakabilimiyini?**

AIRPORTS *(havaalam)*

Most air travelers to Turkey will arrive at Atatürk Airport in İstanbul. From North America, Turkish Airlines (THY) provides nonstop service between Chicago, Miami, or New York and İstanbul, and Delta provides nonstop service from New York. Travelers from North America can also fly nonstop to another city on an airline's major European hub and continue on to İstanbul from there; major airlines serving İstanbul with connections in Europe include Air Canada, Air France, Alitalia, British Airways, KLM/Northwest, Lufthansa, Olympic, Sabena, SAS, Swissair, and United.

Atatürk Airport is 25 km (15 miles) southwest of the city and comprises two terminals, one for international flights and another for domestic flights; a shuttle service connects the terminals. The new international terminal houses restaurants, lounges, and duty-free shops (where prices are listed in Deutsch Marks).

Half-hourly bus service runs from 5:30–10am and 2–8pm, with hourly bus service at other times up to 11pm, and connects both terminals to several stops in the city center, with a final stop near Taksim Square; the bus also makes a stop near Sultanahmet. The city's metro system is scheduled to soon reach the airport, though the opening date of the airport line has not been announced. A taxi ride from the airport to Sultanahmet or Taksim takes about 45 minutes and costs around US$12. You can also make the trip by dolmuş, a less expensive, shared taxi.

A second airport, Sabiha Gokcen, began receiving a limited number of international charter flights in spring 2001 and is expected to expand its operations over the next five years; however, most carriers will continue to use Atatürk airport for the time being.

If you are planning to bypass İstanbul and limit your travels to other regions of Turkey, you may want to consider flying directly into one of the country's other international airports. Two other major airports are those at İzmir, serving the Aegean Coast resorts, and Antalya, serving the Mediterranean Coast. Nonstop flights from London, Paris, Frankfurt, and other European cities into these airports generally operate in summer only with once- or twice-a-week service. These airports are also served by charters in summer.

Domestic flights, primarily on Turkish Airlines, connect İstanbul with airports throughout the country. If you are continuing on from İstanbul to other areas, you may want to consider flying to İzmir or Bodrum for towns on the Aegean Coast; to Dalaman or Antalya for towns on the Mediterranean Coast; and to Kayseri for towns in Cappadocia.

B

BICYCLE AND MOPED RENTAL

With its summer heat and the poor condition of many roads, Turkey is not kind to bicyclists. While you may find bicycles for rent in some of the larger coastal resorts and in Cappadocia, you are far more likely to come upon outlets that rent mopeds and scooters. Except in a few confined areas crisscrossed with small, easily navigated roads, such as the Bodrum Peninsula and Cappadocia, you will probably find that travel on even a motorized bike can be rough going. For instance, even a relatively short ride from one Mediterranean coastal resort to another can be a harrowing experience along the winding, pot-holed, traffic-dense coast highway. If you do rent a motorized bike, expect to provide a driver's license, make sure the rates include insurance, and insist on being provided with a helmet (and wear it at all times).

BUDGETING FOR YOUR TRIP

Good news: Turkey is relatively inexpensive, and even when you do pay a lot for a hotel room or meal, you will probably find that you get far more for your hard-earned money than you do at home or in many other places you might travel.

When determining your budget, think of İstanbul and a few of the major resorts, such as Bodrum, and the rest of Turkey as two separate entities. İstanbul, on this scale, is moderate in terms of cost, while the rest of the regions are inexpensive. In İstanbul or Bodrum, for example, you can expect to pay $100 for very comfortable double accommodations. Elsewhere, you can probably find the same room for about half that amount.

Meals are not terribly expensive anywhere in Turkey, except in some of the finest restaurants in İstanbul, where two can eat very well for $50 or so; expect to pay a fraction of that in most eateries, however. A light lunch, admission to archaeological sites, bus fares, coffee and other drinks are all quite inexpensive, often little more than $1.

C

CAMPING (kamping)

Camping is permitted only at designated sites, of which there are relatively few in Turkey. Many of these are along the Aegean and Mediterranean coasts, and are open from April through October. Local tourist offices often provide camping information in their accommodations listings, since many campgrounds are located on the grounds of pansiyons, For a list of camp sites, including those managed by the forestry department, national park service, and other government agencies, contact: Turkiye Kamp ve Karavan Dernegi (Turkish Camp and Caravan Association), Bestekar Sok No. 62/12 Kavaklidere, Ankara; Tel. 312-466-19-97; fax 312-426-85-83.

An unusual way to enjoy the outdoors while succumbing to a modicum of creature comforts is to stay in one of the treehouses that are common along the Mediterranean Coast, especially around Olympos. These are often just covered sleeping platforms elevated on stilts (out of harm's way from serpents and other crawling creatures), and are sometimes equipped with such amenities as sleeping mats and mosquito nets.

CAR RENTAL *(araba kiradama)*

Many major companies (Avis, Budget, and Hertz) have outlets in Turkey and provide very competitive rates, especially for rentals of a week or more. If you shop wisely, for example, you may find rates of $250 a week for a small car with standard transmission. Expect to pay considerably more (often double) for a car with automatic transmission and air-conditioning.

Given the country's excellent bus service, you may well want to rent a car on the spot only for a day or two for excursions to out-of-the-way sights of interest. You'll find any number of car rental agencies in all the major resorts, though you should expect to pay more per day than you would on a weekly basis. Try to avoid any agency that charges per kilometer, as rates can climb rapidly, and also be wary of some local agencies that demand that you turn over your passport for the duration of the rental.

While most companies provide basic insurance that covers damage to the vehicle you are driving, collision damage waiver (CDW, which covers damages incurred to other vehicles) is usually not included — you should definitely pay the extra fee for this coverage, as accidents are not uncommon in Turkey (see Driving). A value-added tax of 15% is added to all car rentals, and a surcharge may be applied if you pick up your car and drop it off at the airport. Very important: If you do have an accident when driving a rental car in Turkey, notify the police immediately, because insurance claims are invalid unless accompanied by a police report and the agency is allowed to charge you for damages even if you have taken out insurance.

CLIMATE

Turkey is given to great extremes of climate. Expect high summer temperatures everywhere, cold, damp winters in İstanbul and Cappadocia (where, as elsewhere in Central Anatolia, it can be bitterly cold and snowy), and mild winters on the Mediterranean and Aegean Coasts.

Turkey

Especially pleasant times to visit Turkey are the spring and fall, when temperatures are moderate and crowds are thin.

For İstanbul:	J	F	M	A	M	J	J	A	S	O	N	D
°C max	8	9	11	16	21	25	28	28	24	20	15	11
°C min	3	2	3	7	12	16	18	19	16	13	9	5
	J	F	M	A	M	J	J	A	S	O	N	D
°F max	46	47	51	60	69	77	82	82	76	68	59	51
°F min	37	36	38	45	53	60	65	66	61	55	48	41

For Ankara:	J	F	M	A	M	J	J	A	S	O	N	D
°C max	4	6	11	17	23	26	30	31	26	21	14	6
°C min	-4	-3	-1	4	9	12	15	15	11	7	3	-2
	J	F	M	A	M	J	J	A	S	O	N	D
°F max	39	42	51	63	73	78	86	87	78	69	57	43
°F min	24	26	31	40	49	53	59	59	52	44	37	29

For İzmir:	J	F	M	A	M	J	J	A	S	O	N	D
°C max	13	14	17	21	26	31	33	33	29	24	19	14
°C min	4	4	6	9	13	17	21	21	17	13	9	6
	J	F	M	A	M	J	J	A	S	O	N	D
°F max	55	57	63	70	79	87	92	92	85	76	67	58
°F min	39	40	43	49	56	63	69	69	62	55	49	42

For Antalya:	J	F	M	A	M	J	J	A	S	O	N	D
°C max	15	16	18	21	26	30	34	33	31	27	22	17
°C min	6	7	8	11	16	19	23	22	19	15	11	8
	J	F	M	A	M	J	J	A	S	O	N	D
°F max	59	61	65	70	79	86	94	92	88	81	72	63
°F min	43	45	47	52	61	67	74	72	67	59	52	47

CLOTHING

Although Turks have become inured to the sight of tourists clad in shorts and T-shirts tromping through their cities, they do not like the practice and will treat you with more respect if you dress as they do — in summer, trousers and short-sleeved shirts for gents, and trousers and blouses, skirts, or dresses for women. Meanwhile, dress is much more casual in the coastal resorts, where shorts and T-shirts are indeed becoming de rigueur; they should not, though, be worn anywhere off the tourist track. Bathing suits, tank tops, brief shorts, and other skimpy attire are not to be worn anywhere other than the beach.

Men and women alike should dress modestly (no bare shoulders and legs) when visiting mosques; women should cover their heads with a scarf. When visiting archaeological sites, you will want to wear sturdy walking or hiking shoes for scrambles up rough paths and a hat and sunglasses for protection against the sun.

From October through April you will need a sweater or two in İstanbul and the coastal resorts, and a jacket in Cappadocia. Only the most expensive restaurants in İstanbul require jacket-and-tie formality, but you will want to dress well, even if casually so, for dinner in better restaurants anywhere in the country.

CRIME AND SAFETY

Turkey is relatively safe, and even in İstanbul crime is rarely more serious than pick-pocketing or purse-snatching; be especially careful in crowded markets. This said, you should be aware of some heists that are increasingly being perpetrated against tourists. These include a scam in which İstanbul cab drivers take your money, substitute it with lower denomination bills, and flash them at you insisting that you have underpaid; to avoid this situation, take note of the money you are handing the driver and call for the police immediately if an argument ensues. Far more serious is someone (usually a man), who will offer assistance with directions, only to lure you to an accomplice who may attempt to mug you. There have also been several instances in which seemingly friendly strangers have slipped drugs into tourists' drinks and stolen away with money and valuables while the victims slept off the effects.

Two of the most serious offenses tourists might commit are possession of illicit drugs or antiquities; both incursions are punishable by stiff prison sentences and are not to be taken lightly.

CUSTOMS AND ENTRY REQUIREMENTS

Citizens of Australia, Canada, and New Zealand need only a valid passport to enter Turkey for stays of 90 days or less. Citizens of the US and the UK require a valid passport and a visa that is obtainable from Turkish embassies and consulates abroad and at entry points into the country; the fee for British subjects is £10 and for US citizens it is $45 and must be paid in American dollars. Visas are valid for multiple entries over a 90-day period; remember, however, that a visa can not be issued for a period that exceeds the length of the validity of your passport, and may not be issued at all if your passport is about to expire.

To facilitate the replacement process in case you lose your passport while traveling, photocopy the first page of your passport and the page on which your Turkish visa has been affixed; leave one set of copies at home, and keep another with you, but separately from the passport. If you wait until you reach the border to obtain a visa, photocopy the visa page as soon as possible and keep it in a safe place.

Turkish regulations permit visitors to bring most personal effects, including 200 cigarettes, 50 cigars, and 2.5 liters of alcohol, into the country duty free. Notable exceptions, not surprisingly, are drugs and weapons. Also keep in mind that in the unlikely case a customs official decides to check your bag upon entering the country, you will raise suspicion (and risk confiscation) if you are carrying more than one camera, CD player, personal computer, video player, or other pieces of electronic equipment (which sell for much more in Turkey than they do in Europe and North America).

Currency Restrictions and the Value-Added Tax. While there is no limit on the amount of currency you can bring into Turkey, you must declare any currency over the amount of the equivalent of $5,000 upon leaving the country. However, it is foolish to take lira out of Turkey, since ongoing inflation devalues the currency almost daily and it is extremely difficult to exchange.

A Value-Added Tax of 15% is added to most purchases in Turkey. In many cases, foreigners can claim a refund for part of this tax on purchases of more than 5,000,000 Turkish lira — providing they deal with retailers who qualify for tax refunds (most will display a certificate from their local tax office); are planning to leave the country within 90 days of the date of purchase; and follow some complex procedures. A merchant must provide you with three receipts and a check, which you can present to customs officials at the airport or other departure point who, when such facilities exist on the premises, will direct you to a customs bank that will cash the check or, having customs officially stamp the receipts as you depart the country and mailing the stamped receipts back to the store within a month of departure, in which case the store will then send a check or arrange a bank transfer within ten days of receiving the stamped receipts. In some cases, retailers will simply refund the tax amount on the premises and deal with the paperwork themselves — this is the easiest way to claim your refund, so don't be afraid to ask.

DRIVING

Turkey's roads are not for the faint of heart. While some major highways, including the country's relatively few four-lane toll roads, are well-designed and well-maintained, many roads are poorly paved, poorly marked and lit, and dangerously curvy and narrow. In rural areas, you are quite likely to come upon flocks of sheep and goats and stray farm animals in the road, as well as slow-moving or stopped farm vehicles. All of these pose an extra hazard at night, especially with the not-uncommon presence of unlit wagons and tractors. In fact, you are well-advised to confine your driving to daylight hours.

Other major hazards are your fellow motorists, who tend to drive fast and often recklessly, especially when passing slower-moving vehicles (which you probably will be), and they often drive cars that are not road-worthy. Two words of advice: Drive defensively. Drive on the right and pass on the left. At intersections and traffic circles (roundabouts), traffic on the right has the right of way.

Drivers from the US, Canada, UK, Australia, New Zealand, and South Africa require only a valid license from their home countries (an international driver's permit is no longer required). Motorists bringing their own cars into Turkey must have an international motor insurance certificate and a vehicle registration document; it is useful as well to have an official nationality sticker displayed in the rear of the vehicle. EU residents should have a green insurance card, which will greatly facilitate matters in case of an accident. Drivers and all passengers must wear seat belts, and motorcyclists must wear helmets. Make sure you car is equipped with flares and a red warning triangle in case of breakdown.

The speed limit on secondary roads is 90km/h (55mph); in towns, it's 50km/h (30mph). In case of an accident or breakdown, dial the Turkish Touring and Automobile Association 24-hour emergency service at 212-280-4449 (your call may well not be answered by an English speaker, so it's helpful to have someone who speaks Turkish at your side). The person who answers the phone can probably help you contact a nearby repair service or the local police and help you make arrangements.

It is usually difficult (and often illegal) to park on the street in towns, cities and busy resorts. Look at signs carefully — parking is often highly restricted. Many cities and towns have parking lots at the fringes of commercial and tourist centers; use these whenever possible.

Gas (petrol) is readily available around larger towns and resorts; however, you should fuel up for long drives between such places, because stations can be far apart and there are few in rural areas. Fuel is inexpensive by European standards and expensive by North American standards — about the equivalent of $1 a liter. It is available in super and normal grades, and lead-free fuel (kursunzuz) is available in larger stations.

Signage is uneven. Some common terms you are likely to encounter (and these will sometimes but certainly not always be accompanied by the international symbol) are:

Durmak yasaktır	No stopping
Yol Yapımı	Men working (road works)
Dikkat	Danger
Yavaş	Slow down
Tek Yön	One-way

Giremez	No entry
Şehir Merkezi	Town Center

Some useful phrases:

Driver's license	**Ehliyet**
Petrol	**Benzin**
Petrol station	**Benzin istasyonu**
Oil	**Motor yagi**
Tire	**Lastik**
Brakes	**Frenler**
It does not work.	**Calismiyor**.
Fill the tank, please.	**Doldurum, lütfen.**
I've had a breakdown.	**Arabam arızalandı.**
There's been an accident.	**Bir kaza oldu.**

E

ELECTRICITY

The 220V/50Hz is standard. Visitors from countries outside of Europe may require an adapter for electrical appliances, as outlets are geared to the plugs with two or three prongs that are used in Continental Europe; travelers from North America will need a converter as well.

EMBASSIES AND CONSULATES

These offices are the places to go if you lose your passport, are embroiled in police or other bureaucratic dealings, or are otherwise in need of assistance. The American Consulate in İstanbul is at Mesrutiyet Caddesi 104-108 Tepebaşi/Beyoğlu, Tel. 212-251-3602; the British Consulate is at Mesrutiyet Caddesi 34, Tepebaşi/Beyoğlu, Tel. 212-293-7540; the Canadian Consulate is at Büyükdere Caddesi, Begün Han, 107/3, Tel. 212-272-5174. British subjects will also find consulates in Antalya, at Kızılsary Mah., Caddesi Pirilti Sitesi, Tel. 242-247-7000; in

Turkey

Bodrum at Atatürk Caddesi, Adliye Sokak, 12/C, Tel. 252-316-4992; and in Marmaris at Barbaros Caddesi 118, Tel. 252-412-6486.

Citizens of English-speaking countries can also turn to their embassies in Ankara.

Australia: Nenechatun Caddesi 83, Gaziosmanpaşa, Tel. 312-446-1180.
Canada: Nenechatun Caddesi 81, Gaziosmanpaşa, Tel. 312-436-1275.
Great Britian: Sehit Ersan Caddesi 46/A, Cankaya, Tel. 312-468-6230.
New Zealand: 13/4 Iran Caddesi, Kavaklıdere, Tel. 312-467-9056.
US: Atatürk Bulv. 110, Kavaklıdere, Tel. 312-468-6110.

EMERGENCIES (also see POLICE)
Call 155 for the police (use this as a general police number; you will be directed to specialized police numbers if necessary); 110 for the fire department, and 112 for an ambulance.

Help!	**Imdat!**
I am ill.	**Hastayım.**
Call a doctor.	**Doktor cagirim.**
Where is the hospital?	**Nerede hastane?**

G

GAY AND LESBIAN TRAVELERS

Although homosexual activity between consenting adults over the age of 18 is legal in Turkey, be warned that Turks are generally not accepting of homosexual lifestyles. In fact, to date, the gay rights movement has met considerable resistance in Turkey, and it remains illegal to print and distribute material that promotes homosexuality. A recent government decision not to allow a gay cruise ship to dock in Turkish ports is perhaps a sign that the country is not ready to accept openly gay behavior among foreigners. At the same time, it is quite common in Turkey for members of the same sex to travel, dine, and otherwise socialize together, so gay couples should feel quite comfortable traveling together.

Although Turkish men often greet each other with a kiss and often make physical contact with one another, openly affectionate and sexually charged contact between members of the same sex is likely to attract attention and could well result in a bashing. The most gay-friendly spots are the larger resorts, such as Bodrum and Marmaris, but even these places fall far short of providing what might be called a "gay friendly" ambiance.

GETTING THERE

By Air

Given the relatively long distances between Turkey and the rest of Europe (İstanbul is about 3,000 km/1,800 miles from London), most travelers arrive by air. If you are traveling from North America, Australia, New Zealand, South Africa, and most European cities, you will most likely fly into İstanbul's Atatürk Airport and make air or land connections from there. İzmir is another option, especially for travelers concentrating on the Aegean Coast, with Lufthansa providing regularly scheduled flights from overseas via Frankfurt. Antalya also handles regularly scheduled flights from Europe (with much greater frequency during the summer season than at other times of the year) and is well situated for travelers heading to resorts along the Mediterranean Coast. (For more information on flights into Turkish airports, see Airports, page 144.)

If you are traveling from İstanbul to other cities in Turkey, you will find that Turkish Airlines (THY) offers the most flights and, to accommodate resort-bound travelers, adds many more to Antalya, Bodrum, Dalaman, and İzmir during the summer season. Within Turkey, you can reach Turkish Airlines at Tel. 212-252-1106. For scheduling and additional contact information, visit the airline's web site, <www.turkishairlines.com>. You will find travel agents selling domestic plane tickets in virtually all towns and cities of any size and even in smaller resorts.

When planning a trip to Turkey, remember that high season (when rates are highest) is from June into early September; shoulder season, when prices are substantially lower than they are in high season, is from April through May and early or mid-September through October; and low season is November through March — with the notable exceptions of Christmas and Easter, when fares return to high-season levels.

Budget Options. In general, the most economical fares are APEX, which usually require an advance purchase of 14 to 21 days and are valid for stays of 7–30 days; fares are almost always lower for midweek departures. The lowest fares are usually available in the slowest travel times — extremely low fares are often available in early November, early December, and January through March. An option that can sometimes save you money when traveling to Turkey from outside Europe is to fly on another European national carrier to its European hub and continue on to İstanbul or another Turkish city from there. British Airways, KLM/Northwest, Air France, Lufthansa, and other European carriers often offer attractive rates on such routing — sometimes allowing a stopover in the country in which they are based — especially out of season.

A few charter carriers also serve Turkey, offering low fares. Most charters to Turkey operate from European cities and serve airports near coastal resorts, such as those at Dalaman and Antalya and are not really a feasible option for non-European travelers, for whom it is probably easier and less expensive to book a regularly scheduled flight to Turkey. Keep in mind that there are many drawbacks to charter travel. Charter flights often depart at inconvenient times. Since charter companies often operate only one or two aircraft, in the case of mechanical problems, you can be stranded for hours. Seating is usually crowded and service is sometimes not up to the standards of other airlines. And since charter companies operate on low margins, they might cancel flights that are not fully booked and, in the worst-case scenario, go out of business, leaving you holding a worthless ticket or stranded abroad.

By Land

While it's possible to travel from other European cities to İstanbul by train, the journey is long (about 72 hours from London) and probably more expensive than a flight. In fact, the only reason you might want to make such a trip is to take advantage of the opportunity to make many stops along the way. If you do travel by train, consider doing so on a money-saving rail pass; see budget options below.

Likewise, it will take at least four days to drive to Turkey from most places in western Europe, and since such hazards as poor roads and troubled political conditions render travel through Serbia, Romania, and Hungary difficult, to say the least, the trip will involve some careful planning. The most expedient route is to drive to Italy and continue from there to Greece or Turkey by ferry.

Budget Options. If you are planning extensive rail travel in Europe with an eastward journey to Turkey, you may want to consider one of the many available types of rail passes. A Eurail pass (available only to travelers who do not reside in an EU country) allows unlimited travel through 17 European countries (the UK and Turkey are notable exceptions, though the pass will get you to the Turkish border) for periods of 15 to 90 days on consecutive passes, and 10 to 15 days within a two-month period on the Flex pass. For more information, contact Rail Europe, Tel. 800-438-7245 in the US; 800-361-7245 in Canada; or visit the website <www.raileurope.com>. Travelers in Australia and New Zealand may want to contact an international rail agency such as Rail Plus, Tel. 1300-553-003 in Australia (09-303-2484 in New Zealand); the web address is <www.railplus.com.au>.

By Sea

Several maritime companies sail from Italy to Turkey, with service from Ancona, Bari, Brindisi, and Venice to Antalya, Çeşme, İstanbul, İzmir, and other Turkish ports. For more information, contact

Turkey

Turkish Maritime Lines in İstanbul, Tel. 212-245-5366. In the UK, contact Alternative Travel Holdings, 146 Kingsland High Street, London E8 2NS, Tel. 170-241-2687. A good source of general information on ferry service to Turkey from Italian and Greek ports is the Sweden-based Ferry Center, <www.ferrycenter.se>.

GUIDES AND TOURS

Agencies specializing in tours of every corner of Turkey abound. Tourist offices, local travel agencies, and hotels can provide lists Good sources of information on tour operators who specialize in Turkey are professional travel organizations: in the US, American Society of Travel Agents, Tel. 800-965-2782; in the UK, Association of British Travel Agents, Tel. 020-7637-2444; in Canada, Association of Canadian Travel Agents, Tel. 613-237-3657; in Australia, Australian Federation of Travel Agents, Tel. 02-9264-3299; in New Zealand, 04-499-0104.

The many tours that bring visitors to the regions include some interesting educational opportunities. A good source of information on learning vacations is the Shaw Guides, available on the Internet at <http://www.shawguides.com>.

Wherever you go in Turkey, you will encounter guides offering their services outside of museums, archaeological sites, and other attractions. While they may or may not furnish enlightenment you wouldn't otherwise come by on your own, these guides can often provide some local insights (not to mention color) and usually charge very reasonable fees. If you are put off by a guide's persistence, don't hire him. On the other hand, if he speaks reasonably good English and seems somewhat knowledgeable, you might take the plunge at least once and determine for yourself if the experience is worthwhile. Don't be put off if at the end of the tour the guide offers to take you to a relative's carpet shop — it is part of the profession.

H

HEALTH AND MEDICAL CARE

No vaccinations are required for travel to Turkey, and travel poses very few risks to health. You are not likely to encounter any unusual strains of infectious ailments, although malaria is still a hazard on the Mediterranean Coast east of Alanya; if you are planning to travel in these far southeastern regions, see your physician about anti-malaria medications. Some other risks include:

Rabies, which is still prevalent in Turkey. If bitten by an animal that could be rabid, seek medical attention with the possibility of beginning a regimen of anti-rabies shots.

Snake and insect bites, especially from scorpions. You should be especially careful when walking through the brush, such as is found in some archaeological sites.

Diarrhea, which often results from food cooked in unsanitary conditions. For this reason, avoid unwashed salads and fruits in establishments that seem as though they may not maintain strict standards of hygiene.

When packing for your trip, include sunscreen and a hat for protection against the sun; it is best to avoid excessive exposure during hours when the sun's rays are strongest, from 10am–4pm. You will also want to include insect repellent. Turkish pharmacies are well supplied with medicines and supplies, and pharmacists are usually very well trained and happy to provide advice or lead you to a doctor. Pharmacies are open during normal business hours; in each town, one pharmacy stays open late and on Sundays on a rotating basis, and the after-hour locations are posted in all pharmacies.

Water is considered safe to drink, though it is heavily chlorinated. Turks prefer bottled water *(suryu),* which is very inexpensive; still water is sise suryu; and sparkling water is maden suryu. Travelers from abroad may want to follow their example: Water pipes in many cities and towns are very old and impurities may leach in, and spring-fed systems in the country can sometimes be contaminated by animals.

Turkey

If you do become ill, many insurance policies (including the US Medicare system) will not cover treatment in Turkey. However, travelers from EU countries are covered by their national policies, and North Americans and citizens of other countries who are not covered when traveling abroad can purchase additional travel insurance (check with your insurance carrier about this optional coverage). You will often be asked to pay for treatment up front, so keep all receipts for reimbursement. A good source for information on health concerns when traveling is the International Association for Medical Assistance to Travelers (IAMAT). In the US, contact IAMAT at 417 Center Street, Lewiston, NY 14092, Tel. 716-754-4883; and in Canada at 40 Regal Road, Guelph, Ontario N1K 1B5, Tel. 519-836-0102.

Where can I find a doctor/ dentist?	**Nereden bir doktor/ bir disci bulabilirim?**
Where is the nearest pharmacy?	**En yakin eczane nerededir?**
Sunburn	**Güneş yanğı**
Fever	**Ateş**
Stomachache	**Mide bozulması**

HOLIDAYS

Turks enjoy year-round festivals (see page 132), and celebrate the following national holidays:

New Year's Day	**1 January**
National Independence and Children's Day	**23 April**
Atatürk Commemoration and Youth and Sports Day	**19 May**
Victory Day	**30 August**
Republic Day (anniversary of the declaration of the Turkish Republic)	**29 October**
Anniversary of Atatürk's death	**10 November**

In addition, important Muslim holidays, such as Kurban Bayrami in early spring and Seker Bayrami in early winter, are celebrated nationwide.

LANGUAGE

While English is spoken widely in hotels and other tourist facilities in resorts and cities, you may well find yourself in many places where English is not spoken. Try to speak at least a few words of Turkish: English-speaking or not, Turks will applaud your efforts.

Among Atatürk's sweeping reforms were his attempts to "modernize" the Turkish language. As a result, sine the 1920s Turkish has been written in the Roman alphabet. Many letters are pronounced as they are in English. Some exceptions:

c like **j** in **j**am

ç like **ch** in **ch**ip

ğ almost silent, lengthening the preceding vowel

h always pronounced

ı like **i** in s**i**r

j like **s** in plea**s**ure

ö like **ur** in f**ur**

ş like **sh** in **sh**ell

ü like **ew** in f**ew**

Some basic words and phrases:

Good morning.	**Günaydın.**	Goon-eye-DEN
Please.	**Lütfen.**	LEWT-fen
Thank you.	**Teşekkür ederim.**	Tay-shake-kur eh-day-REEM
Excuse me.	**Ozur dilerim.**	Oh-ZEWR deel-air-eem
Where is…?	**Nerde…?**	NEH-deer…?
I don't understand.	**Anlamıyorum.**	Ahn-LAH-muh-yohr-um

I'd like…	**Istiyorum…**	EES-tee-yohr-ruhm

Numbers:

bir	beer	one
iki	ee-KEE	two
üc	ooch	three
dört	doort	four
beş	besh	five
altı	ahl-TUH	six
yedi	YED-dee	seven
sekiz	sek-KEEZ	eight
dokuz	doh-KOOZ	nine
on	ohn	ten
yüz	yewz	hundred

Days of the week:

Monday	**Pazartesi**	Pahz-AHR-teh-see
Tuesday	**Salı**	SAHL-luh
Wednesday	**Çarşamba**	Char-shahm-BAH
Thursday	**Perşembe**	Pair-shem-BAH
Friday	**Cuma**	JOON-ahz
Saturday	**Cumartesi**	Joom-AHR-teh-see
Sunday	**Pazar**	Pahz-AHR

M

MAPS

A good map is essential in Turkey, with its many small tracks leading to beaches, archaeological sites, and spectacular wilderness areas. Likewise, a good city map is essential when navigating İstanbul and other major cities, which often sprawl along the routes of ancient streets. While you can find some maps in cities and resorts, you are well advised to arrive with at least a good map of the country in hand. Some of the more readily available are those in the Euro Map series produced by the German company Hallwag.

MEDIA

Some British and fewer American newspapers are available at newsstands in İstanbul and in larger resorts. Another way to keep up with Turkish and world events is through the English-language *Turkish Daily News,* widely available in cities and resorts.

In addition, the government-run Tourism Radio broadcasts news and other programming in English from 8:30–10:30am and 12:30–6:30pm daily. You'll find it on FM bands throughout the country, usually between 100 and 102 MHz. News in English is broadcast on Turkish television TV2 around 10pm daily. Many hotels are now equipped with satellite TV, on which you can find CNN, Sky News, MNBC, and other English-language stations.

MONEY

Currency. The unit of currency in Turkey is the lira, usually abbreviated as TL. Common bank notes are 100,000, 250,000, 500,000, 1,000,000, 5,000,000 and 10,000,000 lira; common coins are 10,000, 25,000, 50,000 and 100,000 lira pieces. Given the enormous sums involved in even the smallest transaction, merchants will often give prices without the zeros, so don't be surprised if something that costs 10,000,000 lira is simply quoted as costing "ten."

Inflation in Turkey is soaring as high as 100% a year, and the lira is continually devalued to keep pace with it. Prices, accordingly, remain relatively stable, despite the enormous sums involved. In early 2002, the central bank plans to introduce a new series of bank notes and do away with the mind-boggling zeros.

Currency Exchanges. Banks are generally open 8:30am–noon and 1:30–5pm, and are usually closed on Saturday and Sunday; very occasionally, a bank in a major resort will open on Saturday morning as well. Major banks in cities and at least one bank in most towns have currency exchanges. Post offices also usually have currency-exchange windows, and many local travel agencies, especially those in popular tourist areas, exchange money. Remember that it is very difficult to exchange Turkish lira once you leave the country, and inflation renders it less valuable every day you hold on to it; therefore, plan to leave the country with as few lira as possible.

Travelers' Checks and Credit Cards. Both are widely accepted, though most establishments give an unfavorable exchange rate on travelers' checks; you are better off cashing them at a currency exchange and paying in cash. Visa and Master Card are the most widely accepted credit cards, and many establishments do not take American Express cards.

ATM Machines. These technological advances make traveling much easier. Using your bank card, you can withdraw money all over the world in the local currency, usually at exchange rates that are more favorable than those you would receive at a currency exchange. ATM machines, which offer instructions in English, sprout from the sides of buildings in even smaller Turkish towns and resorts these days. However, malfunctioning communications systems with central banks often render ATMs outside of major cities useless, so plan accordingly and try to use them only when a backup is available.

OPEN HOURS

In general, hours are: archaeological sites, 8am–6pm daily (with many variations); banks, 8:30am–noon and 1:30–5pm, Monday–Friday; government offices, 8:30am–12:30pm and 1:30–5:30pm, Monday–Friday (tourist offices are often open on weekends as well; see page 170); museums, 9:30am–5:30pm Tuesday–Sunday (with many variations); restaurants, noon–2:30 or 3pm for lunch, 7 or 7:30pm–10 or 10:30pm for dinner (those that have music and offer drinks will sometimes remain open into the small hours); shops, 9:30am–7pm (as late as midnight during the summer season in some resorts).

P

POLICE *(polis)*

There are many kinds of police in Turkey: *Polis* deal with petty crime, traffic, parking, and other day-to-day matters (including the concerns of tourists asking for directions); *Jandarma,* the highly trained national force, actually a branch of the army, handle serious crime and civilian unrest, protect government figures, and perform other high-profile tasks; *Trafik Polis* monitor the streets of larger towns and cities; *Belediye Zabıtası,* the market police, patrol market areas with an eye out for shoplifters and dishonest merchants; and *Turizm Polis,* who often speak English, are on hand in busy tourist areas. To reach the police, in whatever guise, dial 155.

Where's the nearest police station?   **En yakim karakol nerede?**

POST OFFICES

Turkish post offices are easily recognized by their PTT signs. In major cities, the central post office is open from 8am–midnight; others are open from 8:30am–12:30pm and 1:30–5:30pm. Aside from providing a range of postal services, post offices also offer telephone and fax services and often currency exchanges.

Postage rates change all the time to keep pace with inflation, but it costs roughly about 70 cents to air mail a postcard or letter weighing up to 20 grams to the US, the UK, Australia, New Zealand, or South Africa. Express service is costly but very fast, with next- or second-day delivery to the UK and even the US for about $18.

PUBLIC TRANSPORTATION

A good network of public transportation — usually by bus and dolmuş (shared taxi) — makes it easy to move between major cities and towns in Turkey without a car, though having your own transportation makes it much easier to set your own schedule. Even remote archaeological sites and beaches are usually connected to nearby towns by public transportation, but service can be infrequent.

Tourist offices sometimes provide bus schedules and fare information; in fact, if you explain where you want to go and when, the staff might look up times for you. Any town of any size also has a centrally located otogar (bus station) that is the hub of local and long-distance transportation. Schedules are posted prominently, though each bus company will post its own, so you will have to do some comparison shopping.

Large towns and cities are served by local buses; buy tickets at kiosks before boarding. A dolmuş fleet (often vans) also operates in most towns and often serves as the main transport between smaller villages off major bus routes as well; they ply established routes and will drop off passengers upon request along the way. Stops are marked with a "D." In resorts, a dolmuş often provides fast and inexpensive transport to a beach, and you can usually catch a dolmuş from a town to a nearby, outlying archaeological site or other major attraction. A fleet of yellow taxis also serves most larger towns; make sure the meter is running, that the driver understands where it is you want to go, and that you are given an idea of the fare before you set off. Whatever you're quoted, you'll probably pay a lot less than you would for a taxi ride in many other places.

Long-distance buses, many of which travel by night, are often the only mode of transportation available between cities and towns within Turkey (train service is sparse, and only the major rail lines connect İstanbul and Ankara). Coaches tend to be clean, comfortable, and reliable, and since many companies often ply the same routes, the biggest discomfort you are likely to encounter is determining which bus to take. Companies have offices at the otogars and sometimes in main business districts; when purchasing tickets, you are better off doing so at the otogar, since you can easily walk from office to office to compare timetables. Don't expect to get to your destination speedily — buses stop for frequent rest and meal stops. Do, however, expect to pay very little for the trip — about $20 for the long haul from Antalya on the Mediterranean Coast all the way up to İstanbul.

When is the next bus to…?	**Bir sonraki otobüs kaçta kalkiyor…?**
A ticket to…	**a bir bilet…**
What time does it leave?	**Kaçta kalkiyor?**
How long does it take?	**Ne kadar surebilir?**
How much does it cost?	**Ne kadar?**

R

RELIGION

Turkey is predominantly (99%) Muslim. In İstanbul and some other cities, you may find services of other denominations; tourist offices (see page 170) can provide listings. Non-Muslims are welcome to visit mosques, which are some of the countries most treasured monuments, though they will often be asked not to enter during the five-time-a-day prayers, roughly at dawn, mid-morning, noon, mid-afternoon and sundown. Visitors must remove their shoes (at larger mosques, an attendant will check them; elsewhere, you will usually find a rack inside the door on which you can place them). Men and women should ensure their legs and upper arms are covered (no shorts or armless T-shirts) and women should cover their heads.

T

TELEPHONE *(telefon)*

Public phones in Turkey are usually blue, located all over cities and towns, and take tokens or phone cards, available at post offices and at newsstands. Phone cards come in 30-, 60- and 100-unit denominations. Calls are very inexpensive in Turkey, only a few cents for a local call. To use public phones, pick up the receiver, insert the token or the phone card, and dial the number you wish to reach when the light on the phone goes off, indicating you have credit in the machine.

Turkey

When dialing from city to city in Turkey, you must precede the number with a zero and the city code (for instance, when calling European İstanbul from elsewhere in Turkey, dial 0212); however, you do not dial a city code when calling within that city (for example, drop the 0212 when calling from a number in European İstanbul to another number in European İstanbul). To call internationally, you must first dial 00, then the country code (1 for the US and Canada, 44 for the UK, 353 for the Republic of Ireland, 61 for Australia, 64 for New Zealand, 27 for South Africa), then the city or area code, then the number.

Some hotels apply large surcharges to long-distance calls. One way around this is to use a telephone calling card and bill all calls to that. Your calling card company can supply the access code you must dial to reach its system; simply dial the code, and an English-speaking operator will come on to assist you or you can follow a series of English-language prompts. You can also buy a prepaid international phone card at some newsstands; you will be instructed, in English, to dial a toll-free access number, enter your PIN (which is printed on the card) and then to dial the number you wish to reach; the rates you pay when using these cards are often quite low.

For directory assistance in Turkey, dial 118.

TIME ZONES

Turkey is two hours ahead of Greenwich Mean Time (GMT), which places it two hours ahead of London, seven hours ahead of New York, ten hours ahead of Los Angeles, two hours behind Johannesburg, nine hours behind Sydney, and eleven hours behind Auckland. Turkey switches to daylight saving time in April and reverts to standard time in October.

New York	London	**Turkey**	Sydney	Los Angeles
5am	10am	**noon**	8pm	2am

TIPPING

Tips provide many Turks with a good share of their income. In a country where wages and prices are very low compared to what most travelers are probably used to, a little largesse is in order. Dollars, Euros, and Pounds are much appreciated in this country where the currency devaluates daily, and you will not offend if you leave a tip in these "harder" currencies; a stack of dollar bills is especially handy for tipping purposes.

A service charge of 15% is added to most restaurant bills, but even so it is nice to leave a little extra for good service — the amount depends on the total amount of the bill and the quality of the service, but anywhere from 10–15% is in order; when in doubt, leave a dollar or two. Tip bellhops a dollar or two for carrying your bags, and leave that much per day of your stay for a hotel chamber maid. In many small hotels and pansiyons, the desk staff does double duty as cleaners, room service attendants, breakfast waiters, tour arrangers, and all-around service providers, and it is nice to leave a generous tip upon departure, especially if you've enjoyed an extended stay — $20 or so if the staff has been helpful. To tip a taxi driver, simply round up the total, but be generous — 850,000TL becomes 1,000,000TL, for example. Tour guides, excursion boat operators, and other tourist providers also expect a tip; leave what you want commensurate with the quality of service provided, but $5 or $10 is not out of line as a tip for a day of friendly service.

TOILETS *(tuvalet)*

Public restrooms can be hard to find, and when you do locate one, you often have to pay to use it. Public facilities are often well-maintained, though the toilets are "Turkish" (a basin imbedded in the floor, requiring some maneuvering to which many travelers may not be accustomed). Since Muslim custom calls for cleansing with running water, many public facilities are not equipped with toilet tissue; instead, there is usually a tap and small basin next to the toilet. You may want to carry toilet tissue with you. Note, too, that in many places you will be asked not to flush paper but to deposit it in a basket next to the toilet.

Hotels, better restaurants, some large museums and archaeological sites, and some larger tourist-oriented cafés sometimes have clean public facilities that are equipped with sit-down toilets and tissue; if in need of Western-style plumbing, you might want to seek out one of these. The gents' restroom is designated by **baylar**, the ladies' by **bayanlar**.

Where are the toilets?   **Tuvaletler nerede?**

TOURIST INFORMATION

The place to go first for information is one of the Turkish Tourist Information offices in your home country. They can supply listings of accommodations, sightseeing attractions, tours, and a wealth of other information. Locations are:

Australia: Level 3, 428 George Street, Sydney NSW 2000; Tel. 92-23-30-55.

Canada: Constitution Square, 360 Albert Street, Suite 801, Ottawa, Ontario K1R 7X7; Tel. 613-230-8654; fax (613) 230-3683.

UK: 170-173 Piccadilly, London W1V 9DD; Tel. 170-629-7771; fax 0170-491-0773.

US: 821 United Nations Plaza, New York, NY 10017; Tel. 212-687-2194. 1717 Massachusetts Avenue, Washington, D.C.; Tel. 202-429-9844.

You can also obtain a wealth of information from the government tourism website <www.turkey.org>.

Tourist offices in Turkey can often provide more detailed information, such as listings of local events, that is often not available from tourist offices abroad. If you know in advance which cities and towns in Turkey you will be visiting, you may want to write ahead for an information packet or to obtain specific information. Addresses of some tourist offices in often-visited towns are: Tonguç Caddesi, TRT yani, 11, **Antalya;** Baris Meydanı, Bodrum; Iskele Meydani 8, **Çeşme;** Talatpaşa Caddesi 76, **Edirne;** Mesrutiyet Caddesi 57, **İstanbul** (other offices on

Sultanahmet Square and elsewhere); GOP Bulv. 1/1 Efes Oteli, **İzmir;** Cumhuriyet Meydanı 5, **Kaş;** Mevlana Caddesi 65, **Konya;** Iskele Meydanı 2, **Marmaris;** Agora Caddesi 35, **Selçuk;** Park Ici, **Ürgüp.**

WEIGHTS AND MEASURES
Turkey uses the metric sysyem.

Length

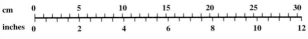

Weight

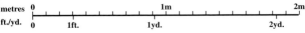

Temperature

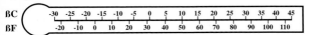

YOUTH HOSTELS
The hostel scene in Turkey is a bit dire — a term that applies to the scarcity of hostels as well as to the surroundings in which you will find yourself when you do locate one. Besides, with the plentitude of inexpensive hotels and pansiyons in Turkey, you probably won't save much money staying at one. If you are intent upon enjoying the hosteling experience, contact the local tourist offices for the nearest locations.

Recommended Hotels

Our selective list of hotels includes only those that we believe will in some way enhance your travels in Turkey. A hostelry we select may have a good amount of character, be well located, provide excellent value for the price, be unusually well-equipped with amenities, or in some other way be above the ordinary. We welcome your contributions on lodgings that you particularly enjoy. Reservations are essential in better hotels almost anywhere from May through September, and are highly recommended at other times.

As a basic indication of what you can expect to pay, we use the symbols below to indicate prices for a double room with bath, including breakfast — but remember that prices may vary with the season. Because the Turkish lira devalues so rapidly, we use US dollars to provide the best estimate of the price.

$	Below $50
$$	$50–$80
$$$	$80–$125
$$$$	$125–$200
$$$$$	Above $200

İSTANBUL AND SURROUNDINGS

Çirağan Palace $$$$$ *Çirağan Cad. 84, Beşiktaş, 80700 İstanbul; Tel. (212) 258-3377; fax (212) 259-6686.* The most luxurious hotel in İstanbul is indeed a palace, built for the last of the Ottoman sultans alongside the Bosporus. Only 12 very opulent suites occupy the original palace; other rooms, equipped with all modern amenities, face the riverside gardens and swimming pool from a new wing. Ongoing renovations are replacing the rather generic room décor with Ottoman-style furnishings of far greater character, adding one more touch to the quite extraordinary experience of staying here. 315 rooms. Major credit cards.

Four Seasons Hotel $$$$$ *Tevkifhane Sok. 1, Sultanahmet, İstanbul 34490; Tel. (212) 638-8200; fax (212) 638-8530.* One of the most luxurious hotels in İstanbul is also one of the most unusual — it occupies a former prison. The luxurious guest rooms, beautifully appointed with kilims and handsome furniture and equipped with lovely baths, face the former prison yard or look out on the Sea of Marmara. Amenities include a glass-roofed restaurant and a health club. 65 rooms. Major credit cards.

Galata Residence $$$$ *Felek Sok. 2, Bankalar Cad., Galata 80020 İstanbul; Tel. (212) 245-0319; fax (212) 244-2323.* Occupying a late-19th-century apartment house near the Galata Tower, this fine, character-filled hotel offers roomy one- and two-bedroom suites with kitchenettes, ideal for families. An old-world atmosphere prevails, and suites are nicely augmented with such comforts as air-conditioning and modern baths. 15 suites. Major credit cards.

Pera Palace $$$$ *Meşrutiyet Cad. 98, Tepebaşı, 80050 İstanbul; Tel. (212) 251-4560; fax (212) 251-4089.* İstanbul's oldest hotel was built in the last days of the 19th century to billet Orient Express passengers. The décor and graciousness of those bygone days prevail, and, even though some of the large, airy guest rooms could use a fresh coat of paint, most guests find that the worn furnishings, ancient baths, the creaky birdcage elevator, and ornate public rooms are a delightful throwback to the last days of the Ottoman Empire. After all, the surroundings have proven acceptable to the likes of Mata Hari and Greta Garbo. 145 rooms. Major credit cards.

Turkey

Yeşil Ev $$$$ *Kabasakal Cad. 5, Sultanahmet, İstanbul 34400; Tel. (212) 517-6786; fax (212) 517-6780.* The most pleasant and character-filled of the Touring and Automobile Club hotels in Sultanahmet occupies a former mansion on a quiet street near the sights of the old city. Rooms vary in size, so you will want to ask for one of the larger ones; all are decorated with old bedsteads, turn-of-the century armoires, and other unique furnishings. Most face a leafy and quiet rear garden; the one suite has its own Turkish bath. 19 rooms. Major credit cards.

Ayasofia Pansiyanlaı $$$ *Soğukçeşme Sok., Sultanahmet, İstanbul 34400; Tel. (212) 513-3660; fax (212) 513-3668.* One of several Touring and Automobile Club hotels in Sultanahmet occupies a row of restored wooden houses next to Topkapı Palace. Guest rooms are small, but nicely appointed with brass beds and other distinctive 19th-century pieces. 57 rooms. Major credit cards.

Konuk Evi $$$ *Soğukçeşme Sok., Sultanahmet, İstanbul 34400; Tel. (212) 513-3660; fax (212) 513-3669.* Adjacent to and under the same attentive management as the Ayasofia Pansiyanlari, this ornately furnished Ottoman mansion offers a much more intimate atmosphere as well as an airy garden. 12 rooms. Major credit cards.

Hotel Empress Zoë $$ *Akbryık Cad., Adliye Sok. 10, Sultanahmet, İstanbul 34400; Tel. (212) 518-4360; fax (212) 518-5699.* The considerable charms of the textiles-filled interior and of the American owner, Ann Nevans, make this small hotel a favorite with return visitors. All of the rooms, reached by a narrow spiral staircase that may be an obstacle to some travelers, are comfortable, but it's well worth spending the extra money for the penthouse, with its large terrace and stunning views of the old city and Sea of Marmara. Reservations are essential. 17 rooms. Major credit cards.

Sari Konak Oteli $$ *Mimar Mehmet Aga Cad. 42-46, Sultanahmet, İstanbul 34400; Tel. (212) 638-6258; fax (212) 517-8635.* Small hotels occupying restored Ottoman houses seem to be opening all the time in Sultanahmet, but this family-run establishment remains one of the most distinctive and most pleasant. Guest rooms are simply but stylishly furnished, and many afford views from small balconies over the Sea of Marmara. The best views, though, are from the rooftop terrace, where breakfast, snacks, and drinks are served. 17 rooms. Major credit cards.

PRINCES ISLANDS

Splendid Hotel $$$ *Nisan Cad. 23, 81330 Büryükada; Tel. (216) 382-6950; fax (216) 382-6775.* If you're in the mood for an atmospheric retreat from İstanbul, look no farther than this wooden, 19th-century inn set in lovely gardens on the largest island of the Princes archipelago. Guest rooms are very large, and what they lack in modern amenities, they make up for with lovely old furnishings and plenty of Victorian-resort atmosphere. Since the Splendid is very popular as a weekend getaway, reserve well in advance. Closed November–March. 70 rooms. Major credit cards.

EDIRNE

Hotel Rüstem Paşa Kervansary $$ *Iki Kapılı Han Cad. 57, 22800 Edirne; Tel. (284) 225-2125; fax (284) 212-0462.* Befitting this city's very long history, the choicest hotel in town dates to the 15th century. While rooms are more functional than opulent, they are quite comfortable and distinctive, and the huge courtyard where camels were once stabled is now a lovely place to relax after seeing the sights. 79 rooms. Major credit cards.

SEA OF MARMARA AND AEGEAN COAST

Behramkale

Assos Kervansaray $$ *Behramkale, Ayvacık 17860; Tel. (286) 721-7093; fax (286) 721-7200.* With its seaside location and lofty ruins, Behramkale is an ideal spot from which to explore Troy, Gallipoli, and other sights along the northern Aegean Coast. This newer seaside hotel is built of stone above a beach and swimming platform and provides the nicest retreat for miles around, with simply furnished but comfortable rooms that enjoy lovely views and easy access to the pleasant little port. 44 rooms. Major credit cards.

Bodrum

Lavanta Hotel $$$ *Yalikavak-Bodrum, 48430; Tel. (252) 385-2167; fax (252) 385-2290.* Crowded, throbbing Bodrum seems, blessedly so, miles away from this picture-perfect retreat that is set in gardens and overlooks the marina and rocky hillside of the still-unspoiled village of Yalkavak. The large airy rooms all have terraces and are tastefully and individually decorated; most of the units are apartments, with well-stocked kitchens. Home-cooked meals are served in a lovely dining room or on the terrace next to the swimming pool. 19 rooms. Major credit cards.

Bursa

Kervansaray Termal Hotel $$$$ *Cekirge Med., 16080 Bursa; Tel. (224) 233-9300; fax (224) 233-9324.* Bursa's most comfortable hotel (at least while the popular Celek Palas is currently being rebuilt) takes advantage of the town's thermal springs to fill a large swimming pool, and a centuries-old hamam provides additional relaxation. The modern and well-equipped rooms are comfortable oases in this busy town, and provide nice views of the surrounding greenery from balconies. 224 rooms. Major credit cards.

İzmir

İzmir Hilton $$$$$ *Gaziosmanpaşa Bulv. 7, 35210 İzmir; Tel. (232) 441-6060; fax (232) 441-2277.* What you might write off as just another member of a big chain has become one of the most talked-about luxury hotels in Turkey. The Hilton, one of several business-oriented hotels in a city devoid of quaint lodgings, pleases guests with its dramatic multi-story atrium, amenities that include a pool and health-club, attentive service, and very attractive, generously equipped guest rooms. 381 rooms. Major credit cards.

Kuşadası

Club Keransaray $$ *Atatürk Bulv. 2, 09400 Kuşadası; Tel. (256) 614-4115; fax (256) 614-2423.* You'd have to look far to find a more atmospheric inn than this, lodged as it is in a 300-year-old rest stop. The courtyard shelters a lovely garden (it can be a bit noisy at night when the adjacent nightclub is in full swing) and rooms are beautifully maintained in their original state, with polished wood floors, fireplaces, and lovely kilims and other textiles. 26 rooms. Major credit cards.

Kismet $$$ *Akyar Me., Turkmen Mah., 09400 Kuşadası; Tel. (256) 618-1290; fax (256) 618-1295.* Long one of Turkey's favored retreats, the Kismet never disappoints, even with the recent passing of the original owner-manager who was a granddaughter of the last sultan. The villa-like hotel is set amid gardens and terraces on a breezy promontory, and guest rooms (most have balconies) either face the busy harbor or open sea. Rooms are quite comfortable though not remarkably atmospheric, but the views, swimming pool, private beach, and friendly service more than compensate for any decorating flaws — and come at a very reasonable price given the quality of a stay here. 96 rooms. Major credit cards.

Pamukkale

Koray Hotel $$ *Karahayıt, 20027 Demizli; Tel. (258) 272-2300; fax (258) 272-2222.* The simplicity of this little inn is quite welcome amid all the gimcrack tourism of this almost-too-famous thermal retreat. The white-washed rooms are pleasant and quiet, and the terraced falls are close but, with their attendant bus loads of admirers, distant enough to ensure some quiet moments around the hotel's own pool. 35 rooms. Major credit cards.

Selçuk

Kale Han $$ *İzmir Cad. 49, 35920 Selçuk; Tel. (232) 892-6154; fax (232) 892-2169.* As if the location weren't enough — this lovely stone inn nestles against Selçuk's castle — the Kale Han is also beautifully decorated with antiques and curiosities and is set in lush gardens. These, and the swimming pool, are a welcome sight after a day of trudging through the ruins of nearby Ephesus, and you need venture no farther than the rustic restaurant to enjoy an excellent meal. 55 rooms. Major credit cards.

MEDITERRANEAN COAST

Antalya

Sheraton Voyager Antalya $$$ *100 Yil Bulv., 07100 Antalya; Tel. (242) 243-2432, fax (242) 243-2462.* Granted, you may not feel as though you're in Turkey when you settle into one of the large, attractive, and unusually well-equipped guest rooms here, but then again, you may not care. Most rooms in this dramatically designed hotel have open sea views from large balconies, and the grounds are lovely, with running brooks, lush gardens, and a large pool. The hotel shuttles guests to its nearby beach. 395 rooms. Major credit cards.

Marina Residence $$$ *Mermeli Sok. 15, 07100 Antalya; Tel. (242) 247-5490, fax (242) 241-1765.* In recent years hoteliers have been snapping up old houses around Antalya's old harbor and converting them to comfortable inns, and the Marina is one of the best. The courtyard swimming pool is a quiet oasis in this busy city, and bay windows, frescoed ceilings, and kilims and Ottoman antiques render the public spaces and guest rooms romantically atmospheric and comfortable. 42 rooms. Major credit cards.

Belek

Tatbeach Golf Hotel $$$ *Belek; Tel. (242) 725-4080, fax (242) 725-4099.* Belek is a somewhat soul-less, purpose-built resort, but is ideal for vacationers who want to divide their time between relaxing on a sandy beach, golfing, and visiting nearby archaeological sites. The Tatbeach is one of the nicest of the new hotels here, with unusually large and pleasant rooms, three swimming pools, tennis courts, and many other amenities, including a golf course. 305 rooms. Major credit cards.

Kalkan

Kalkan Han $$ *Köyiçi, 07960 Kalkan; Tel. (242) 844-3151; fax (242) 844-2059.* Lovely little Kalkan is just the place to settle into a cozy inn, and with its wood balconies, and whitewashed, wood-floored rooms, Kalkan Han fills the bill. One of the biggest attractions is the rooftop terrace, which affords sweeping views over the harbor and is a gathering spot for the well-traveled guests, many of whom have been returning here for years. Most of the accommodations are small suites. Closed November–April. 10 rooms. Major credit cards.

Turkey

Kaş

Sardunya Otel $ *Hastane Cad, 07580 Kaş; Tel. (242) 836-3080, fax (242) 836-3082.* This little hotel on the seaside street leading from the harbor to the Roman theater is quite typical of the hotels that the Turkish families who vacation in Kaş expect to find — simple but comfortable, unpretentious but friendly. Most of the rooms are in a newer building across the street from the water and have sparse but modern wood furnishings, small balconies, air conditioning, and small baths; a few much older and sparser units are in a seaside building that compensates for its lack of amenities with water views. 15 rooms. Major credit cards.

Marmaris

Grand Azur $$$ *Kenan-Eren Bulv. 13, 48700 Marmaris; Tel. (252) 417-4050; fax (252) 417-4060.* In this busy town with no shortage of well-equipped resorts, this new complex on Marmaris Bay is probably the biggest and best of all. Designed to look like a sleek ocean liner, the Grand Azur faces a generous strip of private beach, backed by palm-shaded gardens beneath which a series of swimming pools curve and ripple. This setting is, not surprisingly, quite appealing to families, as are the special children's programs and every watersport imaginable. Guest rooms are comfortable if a bit dull. 284 rooms. Major credit cards.

Side

Hanimeli Pansiyon $ *Side; Tel. and fax (242) 753-1789.* This lovely, small stone hotel seems a world apart from busy Side, yet it is only steps away from the center on a leafy, seaside lane. The simple rooms provide the basic comforts, as well as sea views, and the lush garden serves as a breakfast room and lounge in good weather. Accommodations as pleasant as this are hard to find in Side, so you are well-advised to reserve. 12 rooms. Major credit cards.

CAPPADOCIA AND CENTRAL ANATOLIA

Göreme

Ottoman House $ *Uzundere Cad. 21, 50180 Göreme; Tel. (384) 271-2616, fax (384) 271-2351.* This old house is one of the most distinctive buildings in Göreme — except for the ubiquitous cave dwellings, of course — and it is run with great care as a hotel by a Turkish/Australian couple. The guest rooms are simply furnished, but are airy and nicely accented with rugs and other textiles that are available for sale in the hotel's shop down the street. The rooftop restaurant affords sweeping views of the surrounding fairy chimneys and the snug Harem bar downstairs is one of Göreme's favorite retreats. 33 rooms. Major credit cards.

Güzelyurt

Karbala Hotel $ *Güzelyurt; Tel. (382) 451-2103, fax (382) 451-2107.* The Ilhara Valley cradles an amazing collection of cave churches, and this village just to the east is beautiful and much less traveled than some of the villages in Cappadocia proper. At its center stands this 19th-century monastery, now converted to an unusually comfortable inn. Most of the rooms occupy the vaulted monks' cells and have been designed as duplexes, with a sitting area on one level and a sleeping loft above. Meals are served in the former refectory, and a swimming pool occupies one end of the tree-shaded gardens. 20 rooms. Major credit cards.

Konya

Otel Selçuk $$ *Alaadin Cad. 4, Konya; Tel. (332) 353-2525, fax (332) 353-2529.* Konya is not a place to find luxurious lodgings, but this simple, modern hotel is about the best in town. It's close to the Mevlâna Museum, likely the reason you're here, and air-conditioning and satellite TV provide a degree of creature comforts. 78 rooms. Major credit cards.

Üçhisar

Les Maisons de Cappadoce $$$ *Belediye Meyd. 24, 50240 Üçhisar; Tel.and fax (384) 219-2782.* These beautifully restored village houses, the creation of a French architect, are not only quite luxurious, but provide guests with the sense of finding their own secret retreat in an extraordinary part of the world. Since the houses sleep six comfortably, they are ideal for families and small groups; they are equipped with kitchens, tastefully furnished, and set in beautifully tended gardens; a gardener tends to your private patch of greenery and the management will stock your fridge before you arrive. The minimum stay is four nights. 2 apartments and 6 houses. Cash only.

Ürgüp

Esbelli Evi $$ *Esbelli Sokak 8, 50400 Ürgüp; Tel. (384) 341-3995, fax (384) 341-3995.* Suha Ersoz, the gracious and helpful owner of this inn situated a short walk outside the center of pretty Ürgüp, goes out of his way to make his guests feel as if they are in a private home. He has lavished a great deal of care in fashioning the atmospheric guestrooms out of several old houses partially built into the hillside, connecting them with terraces and stone staircases and installing attractive and comfortable furnishings. A vaulted, Ottoman-style salon is filled with antiques and fine carpets and is a pleasant place to relax and enjoy tea or cocktails, which are provided free of charge; in fact, guests are welcome to help themselves to snacks in the kitchen, to use the washing machine, and in other ways to make themselves right at home. 9 rooms. Major credit cards.

Recommended Restaurants

In our choice of restaurants we include places that best capture the experience of dining in the different regions of Turkey while covering a range of prices. Resorts tend to offer plenty of eateries, and you'll rarely have a hard time finding a decent meal.

Unless indicated otherwise, these restaurants are open for lunch and dinner and are open daily. As a general rule, they serve from noon or 12:30pm to 2:30 or 3pm, and from 7 or 7:30pm to 10 or 10:30pm; during the summer, many resort restaurants stay open well into the wee hours, if only to serve drinks to vacationing revelers.

Wherever you travel in Turkey, you will usually find excellent and friendly service. You may want to show your appreciation with a tip of 10–15% of the bill, even when a service charge is included.

As a basic guide to what you can expect to pay, we have used the following symbols to give an indication of the price of a full meal, excluding wine and other alcohol.

$	below $10
$$	$10–$15
$$$	$15–$25
$$$$	over $25

İSTANBUL

Asitane $$ *Kariye Oteli, Kariye Cami Sok. 18, Edirnekapi, Tel. (212) 534-8414.* Using recipes taken from the kitchens of Topkapı Palace, the kitchen here prepares spicy, exotic Ottoman dishes that may include, depending on the day and season, lamb with currants, chicken stuffed with nuts and raisins, and spicy, saffron-laced soups. The courtyard setting is lovely, and classical Turkish music provides just the right finishing touch for a memorable meal here. Major credit cards.

Cennet $ *Divanyolu Cad.90, Çemberlitaş, Tel. (212) 513-1416.* This eatery, popular with students at nearby İstanbul University, manages to serve excellent light fare and provide a lively, colorful atmosphere. Seating is at low tables, in the center of which traditionally garbed women prepare delicious crepes stuffed with meat and cheese; a vast selection of mezes are also available, as are a few meat and vegetable dishes, depending on the day. Live music is performed in the evenings. Open late. Cash only.

Cicek Pasaji $ *Isitklal Cad., Beyğolu.* This is not one restaurant but several, clustered under the atmospheric arches of the flower market. Food is served from counters and seating is on benches in the passage; the surroundings may be basic and the offerings rarely more elaborate than meze and grilled lamb or chicken, but the experience is certainly memorable. Cash only.

Darulziyafe $$ *Sifahane Cad. 6, Tel. (212) 511-8414.* In this atmospheric dining room housed in the former soup kitchen of the Süleymaniye Cami, you will eat like a sultan — at least, that's the idea, since the kitchen makes an effort to restore authentic Ottoman cuisine. Major credit cards.

Firat $$ *Çakmaktaş Sok. 11, Kampaki, Tel. (212) 517-2308.* Sooner or later you will probably find yourself enjoying a meal in one of the dozens of fish houses on the sea in Kampaki, and you would be hard put to find better preparations than you will here. Fresh fish is either grilled or baked in spicy sauces, and the selection of appetizers is delicious. Major credit cards.

Kathisma $$ *Yeni Akbıyık Cad., Sultanahmet, Tel. (212) 518-9710.* Like many of the surrounding hotels, this pleasant restaurant occupies an Ottoman house. The polished floors, wall hangings, and colorful divans provide a warm, welcoming atmosphere, and the Turkish dishes are well-prepared. Major credit cards.

Pandeli $$ *Egyptian Bazaar, Tel. (212) 527-3909.* Lunch only. Closed Sunday. This atmospheric restaurant, an İstanbul institution, is reached by small staircase at the entrance to the bazaar. The traditional mezes, stews, and grilled meats are delicious, and are served by attentive waiters who have worked here for years. Cash only.

Sarniç $$$$ *Sogukçeşme Sok., Sultanahmet, Tel. (212) 512-4291.* You will come here for the atmosphere, not the somewhat fussy and not particularly distinctive Continental fare. But there is definitely atmosphere, since this elegantly rustic dining room is set at the bottom of a deep, candlelit Byzantine cistern. Given Sarniç's location near the hotels of Sultanahmet, reservations are advised. Open late. Major credit cards.

SEA OF MARMARA AND AEGEAN COAST

Ayvalık

Canli Balik $$ *On Ayvalık pier.* After wandering through the narrow lanes of the old town and enjoying the nearby beaches, you may well want to enjoy a meal at one of the best fish restaurants on this part of the coast. The fresh local catch is the specialty, and you can enjoy it next to the sea beside the swaying fishing fleet. Cash only.

Bodrum

Antique Theater $$$ *Kibris Sehithleri Cad. 243, Tel. (252) 316-6053.* Reservations are essential at one of the most romantic spots in Bodrum, where you'll dine next to a pool while enjoying views of the town and castle. The menu is a pleasing blend of French and Mediterranean influences, with seafood preparations that are far more elaborate than you'll find elsewhere on the coast. Major credit cards.

Restaurant Han $$$ *Kale Cad. 29, Tel. (252) 316-7951.* The tree-shaded courtyard of this old caravansary is a welcome retreat in this busy resort. Although the prices are a bit steep for the simple surroundings, the grilled fish and kebabs that come to the table are excellent and your meal may well be accompanied by music and belly dancing. Major credit cards.

Bursa

Cumcurul $$ *Çerkirge Cad., Tel. (224) 235-3707.* One of Bursa's most popular restaurants occupies an old Ottoman house in outlying Çekirge. Grilled and baked fish are the favorites among the dishes that arrive at tables occupying every nook and cranny of the atmospheric rooms and, in summer, the delightful rear garden. Major credit cards.

Hunkar Donar Kebab $ *Just off Yeşil Cad., in front of Green Mosque.* While the eponymous specialty here is easy enough to find in just about any restaurant, this eatery is one of the best on the square in front of the city's famous mosque. It's a nice place to stop amid your sightseeing rounds. Cash only.

İzmir

Deniz $$ *Atatürk Cad. 188 (in İzmir Palas Hotel), Tel. (232) 422-0601.* One of the best and most attractive restaurants in this busy city specializes in seafood, prepared in some interesting variations that include a kebab of swordfish and several delicious baked fish and vegetable combinations. Major credit cards.

Kuşadası

Ali Baba $$ *Belediye Turistik Carissi 5, Tel. (256) 614-1551.* With its waterside location, attentive service and excellent dishes, it's easy to see why this restaurant is so popular: One look at the fresh catch displayed by the door and you'll know what to order. Begin any meal with some of the mezes, which are often made with octopus, squid, and other seafood in preparations you don't see in a lot of other places. Reservations are advised; ask for a table with a water view. Major credit cards.

MEDITERRANEAN COAST

Antalya

Kral Sofrası \$\$\$ *Yacht Harbor. Tel. (242) 241-2198.* Most of Antalya's better restaurants are on the cobbled streets that surround the old harbor, and this large restaurant that occupies an Ottoman house is one the oldest and best. In good weather, the choice spot is in the garden, but the indoor dining rooms are handsomely outfitted with antiques; the food that comes to the table centers on seafood, imaginatively prepared and nicely served. Closed November–March. Major credit cards.

Dalyan

Denizatı \$\$ *Iskele Meyd., Tel. (252) 284-2079.* The proprietors of one of Dalyan's oldest restaurants know that the way to please is to make the most of the local surroundings. The waterside tables look out to the dramatically lit rock tombs across the river, and the menu relies on the daily catch that comes into the adjacent dock. Closed November–April. Major credit cards.

Fethiye

Megri \$\$ *Eski Cami Gecidi Likya Sok. 8-9, Tel. (252) 614-4046.* It would be a shame to travel along this coast without stopping in this pleasantly non-pretentious town — and while you're here, enjoy a meal at the best restaurant around. Housed in an old stone warehouse in the marketplace, Megri prepares local seafood in dozens of variations. Major credit cards.

Kaş

Chez Evi \$\$\$ *Terzi Sok. 2, Tel. (242) 836-1253.* Some visitors to Kaş eat here every night of their stay, and you may well be tempted to do the same. The garden setting is delightful, and the food an eccentric and tasty blend of French country cooking and Turkish haute cuisine. Closed November–March. Major credit cards.

Marmaris

İstanbul Restaurant $ *Kemer Alti Cad. 4, Tel. (252) 413-4523.* No one could ever go hungry in Marmaris, where the harbor seems to be one continuous line of serviceable but rather unremarkable outdoor eateries. This tiny and simple restaurant, in a private home on a cobbled lane in the shadows of the fortress, is remarkable, however, because of its wholesome simplicity, with a limited choice of fresh cooked meals served in a homey upstairs room. Cash only.

CAPPADOCIA

Ürgüp

Old Greek House $ *Mustafapasa, Tel. (384) 353-5345.* A short drive from Ürgüp out to this delightful little village rewards you with a home-cooked meal in extraordinary surroundings. The restaurant and simple hotel occupy what was once the home of the Greek mayor, and the frescoes and original paneling are cared for as lovingly as the simple local fare is prepared. The proprietors may let you relax before your meal in the hamam that occupies a corner of the courtyard. Major credit cards.

Somine Café and Restaurant $$ *Main Square, Tel. (384) 341-8442.* The fact that this large restaurant serves some of the best food in Cappadocia is not lost on local families, who often join travelers at the long tables on the terrace looking over the town. The food is hearty and typical of the region, including beef and vegetable stews and clay-oven-baked kebabs. Major credit cards.

INDEX